True Comfort

———— ❧ ————

True Comfort

More Than 100 Cozy Recipes
Free of Gluten and Refined Sugar

Kristin Cavallari

RODALE

For Cam, Jax, and Saylor:
Thank you for inspiring me
to be the best I can be, always.
I love you forever.

Contents

❧

Introduction

Comfort food has always played a crucial role in my life.
I grew up in an Italian family, eating casseroles, pasta, and
a ton of sweets. But unfortunately, both white flour and
cow's milk leave me feeling irritable and lethargic. I became
aware of my food sensitivities in my early twenties, and
since then I've been on a mission to make delicious food
using good-for-you ingredients—nutrient-rich ingredients
that still fluff up and thicken, that are creamy and
comforting, that just taste great while fueling your body,
giving it the natural energy it needs. Quite simply, I learned
how to make healthier swaps for the ingredients I had
grown up eating.

These swaps are as simple as using gluten-free oat flour in place of white flour
that's been stripped of all its nutrients. Did you know that natural sweeteners
contain vitamins and minerals? Meet maple syrup and honey, my two baking
best friends. I don't use any crazy ingredients that you can only find at a specialty
store in the middle of New York City. You'll be able to find everything in this book
at your local grocery store, or if not, then you'll be able to order it on Amazon or
Thrive Market. There was no way I could give up all the food I love. What I came
to realize was that if I made these swaps, I could still eat everything I loved and
my body wouldn't hate me for it—and I wouldn't feel like I was missing out
on anything.

Some of my favorite childhood memories are centered around food. I will always remember my Italian grandma making *pizza fritte* (fried dough—um yeah, yum) for my brother and me when we would stay at her house, or my dad and I making homemade meatballs and sauce every Christmas Eve, and my mom teaching me how to make Thanksgiving stuffing the first time I hosted the dinner in my own home.

Good food can transform us and put a smile on our faces. Some days we just need to curl up on the couch with a big, comforting bowl of pasta bolognese. But in the past, when I indulged like that, I'd feel the effects of a bloated stomach and would be so tired I could barely keep my eyes open. Luckily, with the right ingredients, that's no longer the case for me . . . or for you!

After the response to my first cookbook, *True Roots,* which dealt with mindful eating and the 80/20 lifestyle, I realized there was a definite need for these types of healthier recipes. I believe that most people are like me: we know nothing beats comfort food—that's where the heart is. During the fall and winter months, when we're warm and cozy inside our homes, with our loved ones, food brings us together and helps create lasting memories.

This book is a true representation of how my family and I eat on a daily basis. We don't consume cow's milk, gluten, or anything processed and white (like white sugar, white salt, or white flour). We make substitutions with other types of dairy (buffalo mozzarella, anyone?), brown rice and lentil pasta, oat flour for baking, maple syrup and other healthy sweeteners, plus pink Himalayan salt, which is packed with vitamins and minerals.

I'm not a chef—I'm just a mom who loves to cook. I love food and I'm a health nut, and those two things don't have to be mutually exclusive. If I can make these dishes, so can you. And if I can commit to making this an important part of my lifestyle, you can too (if you *want to really change your lifestyle*). You have a choice every day to live your best life.

With love . . . I hope you enjoy this book as much as I loved creating it.

I was so excited to have the opportunity to partner with Kristin in the kitchen again after the success of *True Roots*. For this book, we both drew inspiration from our own upbringings and the food that brought us joy. These recipes are all about comfort and being with family.

When I was growing up, eggplant parmesan and roasted chicken were two of my favorite comfort foods. My mom would make big platters and serve them family-style for all of us to enjoy. It was more than just the food—it was all about being together with family and friends.

Over the course of my culinary education and career, I've cooked many types of food and always enjoyed experimenting with ingredients and trying new, out-of-the-box ideas. You'll find the results here: classic comfort food recipes that Kristin and I modernized to make more health-focused. For example, instead of using ricotta cheese in the stuffed shells, we use cashews, which taste and resemble ricotta almost perfectly. There are so many ways to get creative with alternative ingredients to suit your lifestyle and dietary needs while still maintaining all of the best parts of a dish.

Everyone has a dish or a meal that gives them comfort. I hope you enjoy making the dishes in *True Comfort* on your own or in the company of friends and family, and I hope that they bring back memories of happy times. There is nothing better than the time spent with loved ones while sharing a meal.

Michael Kulisa

Pantry

I believe in real, whole foods, so in my family we try to buy as clean and fresh as possible. We stay away from heavily processed foods. And while the recipes in this book are mostly dairy-free (I never use cow's milk), I do use goat's- and sheep's-milk cheeses and yogurt on occasion (they are easier on the digestive system). The following items are the staples in my house, the ingredients I *always* have on hand so that I'm able to whip up a healthy meal in minutes when I don't have time to run to the store or the energy to go creative. I know I can count on these ingredients to get me through a meal.

ON THE COUNTER

Tons of fresh fruits and vegetables such as bananas, berries, kale, onions, shallots, avocados, tomatoes, and garlic. Multiple kinds of peppers, especially jalapeños—be careful when handling. I try to stick to whatever is in season, especially with fruit—I find you can really taste the difference.

IN THE FRIDGE

Wild-caught fish such as salmon, sea bass, and halibut

Grass-fed bison and beef

Pasture-raised organic chicken

Organic, pasture-raised eggs: we have a chicken coop, so free-range organic eggs are readily available

Fruits and veggies: lemons, limes, zucchini, green beans, spinach, lettuce, apples, cucumbers, carrots, broccoli, and cauliflower

Raw almond butter

Goat's-milk cheddar cheese

Manchego cheese

Buffalo mozzarella

Goat's- or sheep's-milk yogurt

Mayo: I like mine made with avocado oil

Vegan mayo: I use Just Mayo brand

Goat's-milk butter

Fresh herbs, such as thyme, rosemary, cilantro, parsley, and basil

Pure maple syrup

IN THE FREEZER

Bananas: To freeze bananas, peel then store in a ziplock bag in the freezer up to 1 month.

Cauliflower: If you can't find frozen cauliflower at your local store, you can steam florets, then chop and store in a ziplock bag in the freezer for up to 1 month.

Berries, such as raspberries, strawberries, blackberries, and blueberries

Spinach

IN THE PANTRY

Nuts: I like raw almonds and raw cashews, unsalted

Pasta: I use brown rice pasta and lentil pasta

Oils: extra-virgin olive oil, avocado oil, virgin coconut oil

Salt: pink Himalayan salt

Dried herbs and spices: smoked paprika, garlic powder, ground black pepper

Raw honey

Canned coconut milk: both the full-fat and "simple" versions

Canned coconut cream

EQUIPMENT

Vitamix blender

Food processor

Microplane zester

Nut milk bag—can be ordered on Amazon if your local grocery store doesn't carry them.

Crock-pot

Spiralizer

Mornings

Slow-Cooker Banana Bread Oatmeal

The slow cooker will always have my heart. What's not to love about throwing a bunch of ingredients together and essentially forgetting about them? This oatmeal is incredibly creamy, and the bananas will leave a sweet taste in your mouth all day long. Since it is made in the slow cooker, you'll need to take a few minutes the night before to get it going. The best part is, come morning, all you have to do is stir in the maple syrup. Music to a mom's ears! **Serves 6**

2 cups gluten-free rolled oats

4 cups full-fat coconut milk

2 bananas, sliced

1 teaspoon pure vanilla extract

2 teaspoons ground cinnamon

Pink Himalayan salt

2 tablespoons pure maple syrup

1 In a slow cooker, combine the oats, coconut milk, bananas, and 2 cups of water with the vanilla, cinnamon, and a big pinch of salt. Stir together, and cook on the low setting for 8 hours.

2 In the morning, or when it's ready to be served, add the maple syrup to the oatmeal. Stir to combine and serve warm.

Quinoa Porridge Bowl

In a world where it seems like there's a new health trend every other day, quinoa consistently shines with its fiber, protein, and amino acids. A nice change to everyday oatmeal, quinoa porridge is creamy and comforting. I use banana, coconut, and nuts here, but I also like almond butter, hemp seeds, and blueberries. Find your favorite combo to make this your own. **Serves 1**

1 cup full-fat coconut milk

½ cup white quinoa

1 teaspoon ground cinnamon

1 teaspoon pure vanilla extract

1 teaspoon pure maple syrup

½ cup chopped banana (optional)

¼ cup unsweetened shredded coconut (optional)

¼ cup chopped nuts, such as almonds, walnuts, or brazil nuts (optional)

1 In a small saucepan, bring the coconut milk, ¾ cup of water, and the quinoa to a boil. Reduce to a simmer and cook until the quinoa resembles oatmeal and is mushy, about 25 minutes. Remove the pan from the heat, and stir in the cinnamon, vanilla, and maple syrup.

2 Spoon the quinoa porridge into a serving bowl, and top it with the banana, shredded coconut, and nuts (if using).

Apple Dutch Baby

About two years ago, I started waking up at 5 a.m. during the week to work out and get breakfast going before my kids opened their eyes (nothing beats that peace and quiet). Because of that extra time, what used to be a weekend go-to breakfast is now in heavy rotation during the week as well (side note: the only reason it is time-consuming for me is because it takes my oven *forever* to warm up to 450°F). The warm caramelized apples are perfect to keep you and your family cozy on those crisp fall mornings when the fruit is at its best. **Serves 6**

Apple Topping

3 Gala or Fuji apples, cored, halved lengthwise, and thinly sliced

¼ teaspoon ground cinnamon

⅛ teaspoon ground allspice

3 tablespoons coconut sugar

¼ cup virgin coconut oil

Dutch Baby

1 tablespoon virgin coconut oil

¾ cup nut milk, such as almond or cashew

1 tablespoon arrowroot powder

¾ cup oat flour

3 eggs

¼ teaspoon pink Himalayan salt

2 tablespoons pure maple syrup

2 teaspoons pure vanilla extract

1 Preheat the oven to 450°F.

2 **Make the apple topping:** In a large bowl, combine the apples, cinnamon, allspice, and coconut sugar. In a large skillet, heat the coconut oil over medium heat. Add the apple mixture and sauté until tender, 8 minutes.

3 **Meanwhile, prepare the Dutch baby:** Warm the coconut oil in a large Dutch oven over medium-high heat. Once the oil is completely melted, remove the pan from the heat and coat the pan with it, making sure to spread the oil up the sides as well. Set the pan aside on the stove, on the same burner used to melt the coconut oil, to keep warm.

4 In a high-powered blender, combine the milk, arrowroot powder, oat flour, eggs, salt, maple syrup, and vanilla. Blend on high speed until smooth and well combined.

5 Pour the batter into the prepared Dutch oven. Spoon the apple mixture over the batter, making sure to spread it out evenly. Bake until the Dutch baby fluffs up substantially, 25 minutes. Serve right away.

Carrot Cake Pancakes

Grated carrots give these pancakes a nice bite while the cinnamon, nutmeg, and cloves remind me of one of my favorite desserts (yep, you guessed it: carrot cake). Since my kids love pancakes, I'm constantly trying to figure out ways to change them up, and what better way during the fall months than with these warming spices? **Serves 4**

2 large or 3 medium carrots, peeled and grated

1 cup oat flour

1 cup almond flour

1 cup nut milk, such as almond or cashew

1 tablespoon pure maple syrup, plus more for serving (optional)

1 teaspoon baking powder

1 egg

½ teaspoon pure vanilla extract

1 teaspoon ground cinnamon

½ teaspoon ground nutmeg

¼ teaspoon ground cloves

Pink Himalayan salt

Virgin coconut oil, for the pan

Coconut cream, for serving (optional)

1 In a large bowl, combine the carrots, oat and almond flours, milk, maple syrup, baking powder, egg, vanilla, cinnamon, nutmeg, cloves, and a pinch of salt. Stir together thoroughly.

2 Warm the coconut oil in a skillet set over medium heat. Spoon the batter, using about ¼ cup per pancake, onto the skillet and cook for 2 to 3 minutes, until the pancakes start to bubble. Then flip them over and cook for 3 minutes on the other side. Repeat until you have used up all the batter. Top the pancakes with maple syrup and coconut cream (if using), or with your own favorite toppings.

Pumpkin Banana Muffins

In my house, it's not officially fall until the first batch of these muffins has come out of the oven. I like using oat flour since it's light and fluffy. It's also gluten-free, so I don't feel weighted down after eating these muffins. They are gone within a day or two— clearly a house favorite. **Makes 24 muffins**

2 cups oat flour

2 teaspoons baking powder

½ teaspoon baking soda

1 teaspoon pink Himalayan salt

¾ cup pure maple syrup

½ cup nut milk, such as almond or coconut

2 eggs

1 (16-ounce) can pumpkin puree

1½ teaspoons pure vanilla extract

¼ teaspoon ground cloves

2 teaspoons ground cinnamon

1 teaspoon ground nutmeg

2 large or 3 medium ripe bananas, mashed

1　Preheat the oven to 350°F and line a muffin pan with liners.

2　In a large bowl, mix the oat flour, baking powder, baking soda, and salt together until combined.

3　In a blender, combine the maple syrup, milk, eggs, pumpkin puree, vanilla, cloves, cinnamon, and nutmeg, and blend on high speed until completely smooth.

4　Add the wet ingredients to the dry ingredients, and mix well. Fold in the mashed bananas. Spoon the batter, using about ¼ cup for each muffin, into the lined muffin cups. Bake for 25 minutes or until a toothpick inserted in the center of a muffin comes out clean.

5　Let the muffins cool in the muffin pan for 2 minutes, then transfer them to cooling racks for an additional 30 minutes before enjoying them. They keep well in an airtight container at room temperature for up to 5 days, although I've never seen them last that long.

Espresso Overnight Oats

Two of my favorite morning things in one dish: espresso and overnight oats. Take a few minutes the night before a busy morning (or two hours ahead on the morning of) to make this undeniably delicious breakfast combo. **Serves 1**

2 shots espresso, or ¼ cup cold-brew coffee

½ cup gluten-free rolled oats

¾ cup nut milk, such as almond, coconut, or cashew

2 teaspoons pure maple syrup

1 tablespoon chia seeds

1 tablespoon cacao nibs

Toppings of choice (I like shredded coconut and almond butter)

1 Place the espresso, oats, nut milk, maple syrup, chia seeds, and cacao nibs in a mason jar or other airtight container. Give the container a good shake to mix the ingredients, then place it in the fridge for at least 2 hours or up to overnight. If you can, give it a good shake or stir after an hour to mix everything up.

2 In the morning, or when you are ready to eat, stir the oatmeal and then add your favorite toppings.

French Toast Casserole

I had to test this recipe more than any other one in the book because the trick was finding the right gluten-free bread that could absorb the French toast mixture and still be gooey. I ultimately settled on Ezekiel sprouted grain bread, which isn't gluten-free but was the healthiest bread that could achieve the consistency I was hoping for (the gluten-free options I tried were either too soggy or too dense). Ezekiel bread is found in the freezer section at the market, so I leave it on my kitchen counter the night before I make this. If you don't have access to Ezekiel bread, try to find fluffy gluten-free bread—or honestly, just use white bread once in a while and let this be a cheat meal. Just make sure you have about 1½ hours the morning you want to make this—or make it the night before and just warm it up the morning of. **Serves 6**

2 (14-ounce) cans full-fat coconut milk

4 eggs

2 teaspoons ground cinnamon

½ teaspoon ground nutmeg

1½ teaspoons pure vanilla extract

½ cup pure maple syrup

4 cups diced Ezekiel bread (or your favorite gluten-free bread)

½ cup coconut sugar

Cashew Crema (see page 259), for the topping

1 In a large bowl, whisk together the coconut milk, eggs, 1 teaspoon of the cinnamon, nutmeg, vanilla, and maple syrup until combined. Add the bread cubes and toss to coat. Place the mixture in a 13 × 9-inch baking dish, cover, and refrigerate for at least 30 minutes or overnight.

2 When you are ready to bake the casserole, preheat the oven to 375°F.

3 In a small bowl, combine the remaining 1 teaspoon cinnamon with the coconut sugar. Sprinkle this over the French toast casserole until the top is covered with the mixture. Bake for 30 minutes or until the top is golden brown. Let it cool for 30 minutes before serving (the center will set more as it cools).

4 Spoon some Cashew Crema over each piece to serve.

Chilaquiles with Salsa Verde

When we lived in Chicago, every weekend we went to breakfast at
a little hole-in-the-wall place up in the burbs, and I always ordered
chilaquiles. I miss our spot, but when I make this, it takes me back to
those days. I think you'll agree that tortilla chips covered in yummy
salsa and all the fixings make this breakfast bowl both comforting
and hearty. **Serves 4**

Salsa Verde

1 pound tomatillos, husks removed

1 poblano chile, seeds removed

1 small white onion, cut in half

2 cloves garlic

1 tablespoon avocado oil

1 cup chicken stock

½ cup fresh cilantro with stems

1 teaspoon ground cumin

Juice of ½ lime

1 jalapeño with seeds removed
(optional)

1 teaspoon pink Himalayan salt

Freshly ground black pepper

Chilaquiles

2 (7-ounce) packages tortillas
(I like the Siete brand almond flour),
cut into triangles

Avocado oil

Pink Himalayan salt

Freshly ground black pepper

1 large avocado, diced

½ pound cooked, crumbled chorizo

4 eggs, cooked sunny-side up

¼ cup Pickled Red Onions
(page 250)

¼ cup chopped fresh cilantro

⅓ cup Cashew Crema (page 259)

1 **Prepare the salsa verde:** Preheat the oven
to 375°F.

2 On a large baking sheet, toss the tomatillos,
poblano, onion halves, and garlic with the avocado
oil. Roast until browned, about 25 minutes.

3 Transfer the roasted vegetables to a high-
powered blender, and add the chicken stock,
cilantro, cumin, lime juice, jalapeño (if using), salt,
and pepper. Blend until smooth, then set the salsa
aside. (Leave the oven on.)

4 **Make the chilaquiles:** Spread the tortilla
triangles out evenly on 2 baking sheets. Lightly

toss them with avocado oil, and season with
salt and pepper. Bake until the chips are golden
brown and crispy, checking frequently so they
don't burn, 10 to 15 minutes.

5 In a large mixing bowl, toss the tortilla chips
with the salsa verde. Divide half of the chips
among 4 serving bowls, distributing them evenly.
Add a couple pieces of the avocado and chorizo,
then add a layer of the remaining chips.

6 To finish the chilaquiles, top each bowl with
the remaining avocado and chorizo, and place
a sunny-side-up egg on top. Garnish with the
Pickled Red Onions, cilantro, and Cashew Crema.

Shakshuka

If you're like me and love a savory breakfast that's not your typical bacon and eggs, this one's for you. The spicy tomato sauce and the creaminess of the poached eggs make a nice departure from the usual breakfast routine. You can eat it right out of the pan, but I enjoy spooning it into a tortilla and eating it that way. —*Mike* Serves 6

2 tablespoons extra-virgin olive oil

1 medium sweet onion, diced

3 cloves garlic, coarsely chopped

2 cups coarsely chopped kale (stems removed before chopping)

1 green bell pepper, diced

½ teaspoon smoked paprika

1 teaspoon chili powder

1 teaspoon ground cumin

1 teaspoon ground coriander

½ teaspoon red pepper flakes

Pink Himalayan salt

Freshly ground black pepper

1 (28-ounce) can diced fire-roasted tomatoes, with their juice

¼ cup coconut cream

½ cup canned garbanzo beans (chickpeas), drained and rinsed

6 eggs

¼ cup chopped fresh cilantro or parsley

6 tortillas of choice (we like the Siete brand almond flour or cassava/chia flour), warmed

1   In a large cast-iron skillet, heat 1 tablespoon of the olive oil over medium heat. Add the onion, garlic, kale, and bell pepper and sauté, stirring continuously, until the garlic is fragrant and slightly browned, 5 to 8 minutes.

2   Add the smoked paprika, chili powder, cumin, coriander, red pepper flakes, ½ teaspoon salt, ½ teaspoon pepper, and the tomatoes with their juice. Stir together and bring to a simmer. Cook for 10 minutes, stirring occasionally. Then add the coconut cream and cook for 2 more minutes. Stir in the garbanzo beans. Let all the ingredients continue to cook together for 5 minutes.

3   While everything is cooking, preheat your broiler to medium-high.

4   Make 6 small wells in the cooked mixture in the skillet. Crack an egg into each well. Season each egg with salt and pepper, and place the skillet under the broiler. Let broil until the whites of the eggs are firm but the yolks are still runny, 6 minutes.

5   Remove the skillet from the broiler. Garnish the shakshuka with the chopped parsley or cilantro and drizzle the remaining 1 tablespoon olive oil over the top. Serve it hot, in the skillet, with the warm tortillas alongside. Let each person spoon the mixture onto a tortilla, or serve already spooned onto tortillas for each person to enjoy.

Lox Breakfast Bowl

Before I started eating healthy, bagels with lox were my weakness. In high school, I would go to this bagel shop called Shirley's in Laguna Beach and get one at least twice a week. Bagels are so dense and loaded with unhealthy carbs, and cream cheese is made from cow's milk, so between the two ingredients I was a tired, bloated wreck for days. I haven't eaten a bagel in years, but this bowl satisfies my craving. I would actually say it's *better* than the real deal. **Serves 4**

1 teaspoon virgin coconut oil

8 eggs

Pink Himalayan salt

1 cup chopped smoked salmon

6 tablespoons Cashew Crema (see page 259)

1 cup halved cherry tomatoes

2 teaspoons finely chopped fresh chives

2 teaspoons chopped fresh dill

1 teaspoon finely chopped shallots

1 Warm the coconut oil in a skillet over low heat. In a large bowl, whisk the eggs with a pinch of salt. Pour the eggs into the warmed skillet and slowly sauté the eggs until they are cooked through. For really creamy eggs cooked over low heat, this should take around 10 minutes.

2 Spoon one fourth of the eggs into each serving bowl, and add ¼ cup of the smoked salmon, 1½ tablespoons of the Cashew Crema, and ¼ cup of the tomatoes. Garnish each serving with ½ teaspoon of the chives, ½ teaspoon of the dill, and ¼ teaspoon of the shallots.

Banana Bread
with Espresso Cashew Mascarpone

Banana bread will always be one of my favorite baked goods (yeah, me and everyone else). If you aren't familiar with mascarpone, it's a thick, butter-like cheese typically made with cream—but I use cashews, which will make you forget about the real thing. The espresso cashew mascarpone elevates this gluten-free banana bread into something utterly luxurious. **Makes 1 loaf**

Banana Bread

⅓ cup virgin coconut oil, plus more for the pan, melted

⅔ cup coconut sugar

2 eggs

1 cup mashed ripe banana (about 3 small bananas)

2 tablespoons almond milk

1 teaspoon pure vanilla extract

1 cup oat flour

½ cup almond flour

1¼ teaspoons baking powder

½ teaspoon baking soda

¾ teaspoon pink Himalayan salt

¼ teaspoon ground cinnamon

Espresso Cashew Mascarpone

1 tablespoon instant espresso powder

½ tablespoon pure maple syrup

1 cup cashews, soaked for at least 4 hours or up to overnight, drained

½ cup almond milk

½ teaspoon ground cinnamon

1 **Make the banana bread:** Preheat the oven to 350°F. Grease a loaf pan with melted coconut oil.

2 In a medium bowl, whisk the coconut sugar, ⅓ cup melted coconut oil, and eggs together. Add the bananas, almond milk, and vanilla; continue mixing until smooth.

3 In another medium mixing bowl, combine the oat flour, almond flour, baking powder, baking soda, salt, and cinnamon. Stir well. Add the dry ingredients to the wet ingredients, a little at a time, stirring until fully incorporated.

4 Pour the batter into the prepared loaf pan and place it on the middle rack of the oven. Bake for 45 minutes, turning the pan around after 20 minutes, until a toothpick comes out clean and the bread is firm. Let the bread rest for 20 minutes before slicing it.

5 **Meanwhile, make the espresso cashew mascarpone:** In a blender, combine the espresso powder, maple syrup, cashews, almond milk, and cinnamon. Blend until the mixture is completely smooth. If it is too thick, add a little extra almond milk. Spread the mascarpone over slices of the warm banana bread.

Low and Slow Eggs
with Manchego and Chives

Technically, scrambled eggs are supposed to take around 10 to 15 minutes to cook; this will make them melt in your mouth. The key is to cook them at a low temperature and take your time, constantly stirring them. Manchego cheese and chives—a flavor that's a cross between garlic and onion—pair perfectly with these velvety eggs. You will never eat scrambled eggs another way again. **Serves 4**

8 eggs, at room temperature

¼ cup coconut cream

1 tablespoon virgin coconut oil

¼ cup grated Manchego cheese

2 tablespoons chopped fresh chives

Pink Himalayan salt

Freshly ground black pepper

1   In a medium to large mixing bowl, beat the eggs with the coconut cream until the mixture is completely smooth and no egg whites are evident.

2   Warm the coconut oil in a large skillet over medium heat. Turn the heat to low, then add your egg mixture. Cook, stirring continuously from the edges to the center, for 10 to 15 minutes, until the eggs are completely cooked. Remove the skillet from the heat.

3   Fold the Manchego and the chives into the eggs, and season with salt and pepper. Serve immediately.

Oatmeal Bowl with Warm Berry Sauce

I could (and almost do) eat this oatmeal every morning. It just hits the spot: warm and comforting, a touch of sweet with the berry sauce, and filling with the protein from the almond butter. Get ready for a good food Instagram pic. **Serves 1**

½ cup gluten-free rolled oats

1 cup almond milk

Pink Himalayan salt

1 teaspoon pure vanilla extract

¼ cup creamy almond butter

1 teaspoon virgin coconut oil

1 teaspoon hemp seeds

1 teaspoon ground flaxseed

¼ cup Warm Berry Sauce (recipe follows)

Pure maple syrup

1 In a small saucepan, combine the oats, milk, a pinch of salt, and the vanilla. Bring to a boil over medium heat. Reduce the heat to low and cook until the mixture is creamy and the milk has been absorbed, 8 minutes.

2 Place the oatmeal in a serving bowl and top it with the almond butter, coconut oil, hemp seeds, ground flaxseed, berry sauce, and a drizzle of maple syrup.

WARM BERRY SAUCE

Makes just over ½ cup

1 tablespoon arrowroot powder

1 teaspoon fresh lemon juice

½ cup fresh blueberries, blackberries, raspberries, or strawberries (if using strawberries, chop them)

3 tablespoons pure maple syrup

1 In a small bowl, dissolve the arrowroot powder in 1 tablespoon of water and whisk to combine.

2 In a small saucepan, combine the lemon juice, berries, maple syrup, and 3 tablespoons of water. Bring to a boil, then reduce to a simmer and cook for 4 minutes. Add the dissolved arrowroot and cook for 5 minutes or until the sauce has thickened substantially.

Oat Flax Drop Biscuits and Gravy

The first time I had biscuits and gravy was in Nashville, Tennessee, during one of my first visits there. I didn't know it at first, but biscuits and gravy are on almost every breakfast menu in the South (you don't see that in LA!). I tried a bite and I instantly became a fan, but I couldn't get on board with the white flour and cow's milk. Here's a healthier version, inspired by the South.

Serves 4 (makes 10 biscuits, and make gravy ahead and keep warm)

Biscuits

1 tablespoon arrowroot powder

1 cup oat flour

¼ cup ground flaxseed

2 teaspoons baking powder

¼ teaspoon pink Himalayan salt

2 tablespoons chilled virgin coconut oil

2 eggs

⅓ cup nut milk, such as almond or cashew

Sausage Gravy

½ pound ground bison or beef

1 tablespoon virgin coconut oil

1 tablespoon finely chopped shallots

⅓ cup oat flour

¼ teaspoon garlic powder

½ teaspoon ground sage

2 cups almond milk

1 cup full-fat coconut milk

2 teaspoons hot sauce of choice, such as Frank's Red Hot

1 teaspoon pure maple syrup

Pink Himalayan salt

Freshly ground black pepper

Make the Biscuits:

1 Preheat the oven to 350°F and line a baking sheet with parchment paper.

2 In a small bowl, dissolve the arrowroot powder in 1 tablespoon of water, stirring until completely combined. Set aside.

3 In a large bowl, combine the oat flour, ground flaxseed, baking powder, and salt. Add the coconut oil to the dry ingredients, using your hands to break the clumps apart. Gradually incorporate the oil into the flour mixture still using your hands until it resembles dry sand, about 1 minute. Add the dissolved arrowroot, the eggs, and the milk to the mixture. Stir with a spoon until just combined. Let the dough sit for 5 minutes for the baking powder to activate.

4 Using about 2 tablespoons of the batter for each biscuit, spoon the dough onto the lined baking sheet, leaving at least ½ inch between them. Make the biscuits as round as possible. Bake until golden brown, 10 minutes.

Make the Sausage Gravy:

5 In a large skillet set over medium heat, sauté the bison in the coconut oil for 2 minutes. Add the shallots and sauté until both are browned, another 6 minutes. Add the oat flour and stir until combined. Add the garlic powder and sage, and stir to combine. Add the almond milk and coconut milk and bring to a boil. Turn the heat down to a high simmer and while stirring continuously, cook until the mixture thickens substantially and has a sauce-like consistency, about 20 minutes. Remove the skillet from the heat.

6 Stir in the hot sauce, maple syrup, and salt and pepper to taste. Let the gravy sit for 5 minutes to thicken even more. (You can add more oat flour if the mixture is too liquid-y or more milk if it becomes too thick.)

7 Place the biscuits on individual plates and spoon the gravy over them. Serve warm.

Green Tea Waffles

My kids live for waffles. When I make these for them, they get a health boost from the spinach (but I leave out the matcha powder). For us grownups, I leave the matcha in because it contains caffeine. We need a little love here and there, too, right? **Serves 4**

1 egg

2 tablespoons virgin coconut oil, melted, plus more for the waffle maker

1 tablespoon pure maple syrup

½ teaspoon pure vanilla extract

½ cup fresh spinach leaves

1 cup full-fat coconut milk

1 cup oat flour

1 tablespoon matcha powder

1 teaspoon baking powder

Pink Himalayan salt

1 Warm a waffle maker over medium-high heat.

2 In a high-powered blender, blend the egg, coconut oil, maple syrup, vanilla, spinach, and coconut milk together.

3 In a large bowl, combine the oat flour, matcha, baking powder, and a big pinch of salt. Add the wet ingredients to the dry and mix well.

4 Grease the warmed waffle maker with coconut oil. Pour about ¼ cup of the batter for each waffle into the waffle maker; cook for 3 to 4 minutes, until the center is cooked through. Place cooked waffles on a plate, and cover to keep warm. Repeat with the remaining batter. Serve immediately.

Pizza Frittata

I love frittatas for their simplicity; they require only a few great ingredients to be delicious, and they take just a few minutes to whip up in the morning before everyone can go off to work and school feeling satisfied. Plus, who doesn't love pizza? **Serves 4**

6 eggs

1 tablespoon almond milk

½ teaspoon dried oregano

¼ teaspoon garlic powder

Pink Himalayan salt

Freshly ground black pepper

1 tablespoon extra-virgin olive oil

1 large heirloom tomato, thinly sliced

8 slices uncured pepperoni

1 cup fresh basil leaves

1 Preheat the oven to 400°F.

2 In a medium mixing bowl, whisk together the eggs, almond milk, oregano, garlic powder, and a pinch each of salt and pepper.

3 Heat the olive oil in a medium cast-iron or other oven-safe skillet pan over medium heat. Pour the egg mixture into the skillet. Once the edges start to cook, remove the skillet from the heat and layer the tomato slices, pepperoni, and basil leaves over the eggs.

4 Bake in the oven until the center is set, 20 to 25 minutes. Let the frittata cool slightly before slicing it. Leftovers (if there are any) can be saved in an airtight container in the fridge for a couple of days.

Recharge Breakfast Bowl

At times, I find it hard to eat "healthy" in the winter months when it's freezing, holiday season is in full swing, and all I want is something comforting. This bowl is great for resetting and getting back on track while still keeping you warm and cozy and your belly full. **Serves 1**

1½ cups chicken stock

½ cup quinoa

Pink Himalayan salt

2 tablespoons plus 1 teaspoon extra–virgin olive oil

3 cups fresh spinach leaves

1½ teaspoons fresh lemon juice

¼ teaspoon Dijon mustard

½ teaspoon raw honey

¼ teaspoon red pepper flakes

Freshly ground black pepper

2 eggs, cooked to your preference (I like them over easy or scrambled)

½ avocado, diced

¼ cup halved cherry tomatoes

1 tablespoon sliced scallions, white and green parts

¼ cup fresh micro greens

1 In a small saucepan, bring the chicken stock to a simmer. Add the quinoa and a pinch of salt; cook for 25 minutes or until the quinoa is fluffy.

2 In a cast-iron skillet, heat 1 teaspoon olive oil over medium heat. Add the spinach and sauté until it is wilted, about 2 minutes. Add the cooked quinoa, stir together, and season with a big pinch of salt. Cook for 5 minutes, stirring occasionally. Transfer the spinach-quinoa mixture to a serving bowl.

3 To make the dressing, whisk together the lemon juice, mustard, honey, red pepper flakes, and remaining 2 tablespoons olive oil; season with salt and pepper to taste.

4 Top the quinoa-spinach mixture with the eggs, then with the avocado, cherry tomatoes, and scallions. Sprinkle with the micro greens and drizzle with the lemon dressing.

Sweet Potato Toast
Three Ways

Whoever thought of using a baked sweet potato in place of bread is a genius! Sweet potato toast has been all the rage the past few years, and if you've had it, then you know why. It is an explosion of flavor in your mouth that will make you keep coming back for more. **Serves 4**

ALMOND BUTTER, BLUEBERRIES + HONEY

¼ cup sunflower seeds

2 large sweet potatoes, baked, then halved lengthwise (recipe for baking potatoes, see page 183)

1 cup almond butter

⅔ cup fresh or frozen blueberries

½ teaspoon ground cardamom

1½ tablespoons raw honey

1 Toast the sunflower seeds in a small dry skillet over medium heat, stirring constantly until golden brown, about 5 minutes. Remove from the heat and set aside in a small bowl.

2 Spread each of the sweet potato halves with ¼ cup of the almond butter, and arrange the blueberries evenly over the butter. Scatter the toasted sunflower seeds over each sweet potato, sprinkle with the cardamom, and then drizzle the honey over the top.

AVOCADO + EGGS

3 large ripe avocados

Pink Himalayan salt

2 large sweet potatoes, baked, then halved lengthwise (recipe for baking potatoes, see page 183)

8 thin slices red onion

2 hard-boiled eggs, thinly sliced

2 teaspoons finely chopped fresh dill

In a small bowl, mash the avocado pulp with a big pinch of salt. To build your toast, first spread the mashed avocado over the cut side of the 4 sweet potato halves. Then place 2 slices of red onion on each piece, followed by the egg slices. Garnish with the dill and a sprinkle of salt.

SMOKED SALMON + DILL CASHEW SAUCE

1½ cups cashews, soaked for at least 2 hours or up to overnight, drained

3 tablespoons chopped fresh dill, plus more for garnish

1 teaspoon fresh lemon juice

½ cup almond milk

4 cloves garlic

Pink Himalayan salt

Freshly ground black pepper

2 large sweet potatoes, baked, then halved lengthwise (recipe for baking potatoes, see page 183)

2 avocados, thinly sliced

4 hard-boiled eggs, sliced

12 slices smoked salmon

2 tablespoons capers

Extra-virgin olive oil

1   In a high-powered blender, combine the cashews, 1 tablespoon of the dill, lemon juice, almond milk, garlic, and a pinch each of salt and pepper. Blend until completely smooth.

2   To assemble the toasts, evenly spread the cashew-dill mixture over each potato half. Arrange the avocado and eggs slices on top, and season with salt and pepper. Then layer the smoked salmon slices on top and garnish with the remaining 2 tablespoons dill and the capers. Drizzle with extra-virgin olive oil.

SMOKED SALMON
+ DILL CASHEW SAUCE

AVOCADO
+ EGGS

ALMOND BUTTER,
BLUEBERRIES + HONEY

Breakfast Sausage–Stuffed Apples

These stuffed apples are salty and sweet and fancy. Make this delicious breakfast for a crisp fall morning for your houseguests or when you want something a little special. **Serves 6**

3 medium Honeycrisp or Gala apples

2 tablespoons extra-virgin olive oil, plus more for coating the apples and for cooking

Pink Himalayan salt

Freshly ground black pepper

6 ounces ground chicken thighs

6 ounces ground veal

1 shallot, chopped

2 cloves garlic, minced

2 tablespoons bourbon

½ teaspoon dried thyme

1 tablespoon chopped fresh sage leaves

¼ teaspoon red pepper flakes

6 eggs

1 Preheat the oven to 375°F. Line a baking sheet with foil.

2 Cut the apples in half lengthwise. Using a melon baller or a spoon, scoop out the pulp of each apple half, leaving an intact shell. Discard the seeds and stems, then chop the apple pulp and set it aside.

3 Lightly coat the inside of each apple shell with olive oil and season them with salt and pepper. Lay the shells face-down on the prepared baking sheet and bake for 10 minutes. Remove the baking sheet from the oven and set it aside.

4 In a large skillet, heat 2 tablespoons olive oil over medium-high heat. Add the ground chicken and veal and cook, stirring, for about 15 minutes, until browned. Add the shallots and garlic, and cook for another 5 minutes.

5 Remove the skillet from the heat, add the bourbon, and then return the skillet to the burner. Continue stirring while the bourbon deglazes the skillet and the liquid evaporates. Add the chopped apple pulp and cook for 5 minutes.

6 Remove the skillet from the heat and stir in the thyme, sage, red pepper flakes, ½ teaspoon salt, and ½ teaspoon pepper; mix well. Let cool for 10 minutes.

7 Carefully fill each apple shell with the stuffing mixture, then return them to the foil-lined baking sheet. Bake until the apples are tender, about 12 minutes.

8 While the apples are baking, fry the 6 eggs to your desired consistency in a lightly greased skillet over medium heat.

9 Remove the baking sheet from the oven, place a fried egg over each apple shell, and serve immediately.

Almond Donuts
with Dark Chocolate Glaze

My kids go crazy for donuts. We still take them to get the real thing most weekends (I let my kids indulge fairly often), but these hold them over in between. Not only are these donuts made with healthier ingredients than typical store-bought donuts, but they are also baked instead of fried. **Makes 6 donuts**

6 tablespoons virgin coconut oil, melted, plus more for the pan

2 eggs

¼ cup coconut sugar

¼ cup coconut cream

½ teaspoon pure vanilla extract

1 cup almond flour

2 teaspoons baking powder

1 cup dark chocolate chips

1 Preheat the oven to 375°F. Grease 6 cups of a donut pan with coconut oil.

2 In a medium mixing bowl, whisk the eggs, coconut sugar, coconut cream, and vanilla together for 5 minutes, until fully combined. Add the almond flour, baking powder, and 4 tablespoons of the coconut oil. Fold everything together until a batter is formed.

3 Place the batter in a piping bag or large ziplock bag with the corner cut off for easy distribution. Evenly pipe the batter into each cup in the donut pan. Bake for 20 to 25 minutes, until the donuts have risen and become dense. Let them cool on a wire rack before glazing them.

4 For the glaze, place the dark chocolate and the remaining 2 tablespoons of the coconut oil in a large heat-safe glass bowl, set the bowl over a saucepan of simmering water (do not let the bowl touch the water), and stir until completely melted and blended. Then remove the bowl from the saucepan. Dip one side of each cooled donut in the melted chocolate until that side is fully glazed. Place the donuts back on the wire rack for the glaze to harden.

Lunches

Creamy Roasted Veggie Pasta Salad

I couldn't imagine life without pasta—it's my favorite comfort food. Discovering healthier alternatives to the usual white flour was a godsend. I like this pasta dish because it gets a good dose of veggies in while still giving you that creamy, indulgent feeling. I like using vegan mayo for its subtle flavor, but feel free to choose your favorite. **Serves 4**

1 medium zucchini, chopped

1 medium yellow squash, chopped

½ medium eggplant, chopped

1 head broccoli, large stems trimmed off, then chopped

¼ cup extra-virgin olive oil

1½ teaspoons pink Himalayan salt

1½ teaspoons garlic powder

1 teaspoon paprika

2 tablespoons plus 1 teaspoon balsamic vinegar

2 tablespoons raw honey

½ cup cherry tomatoes, halved

½ (12-ounce) package brown rice penne pasta

2 tablespoons chopped fresh basil

3 tablespoons vegan mayo

⅛ teaspoon freshly ground black pepper

1 Preheat the oven to 425°F.

2 Place the zucchini, yellow squash, eggplant, and broccoli on a large baking sheet. Sprinkle with the olive oil, 1 teaspoon of the salt, 1 teaspoon of the garlic powder, and the paprika, and toss to coat. Roast until the vegetables are golden brown, 35 minutes.

3 Meanwhile, in a medium bowl, whisk the 2 tablespoons balsamic vinegar and the honey together. Add the tomatoes and let them marinate for 20 minutes. Then drain the tomatoes, discarding the marinade, and set the tomatoes aside.

4 Cook the penne according to the package directions. Drain, rinse, and place the pasta in a large bowl. Add the balsamic tomatoes, roasted veggies, basil, mayo, remaining ½ teaspoon salt, the pepper, remaining 1 teaspoon balsamic vinegar, and remaining ½ teaspoon garlic powder. Mix to combine. Serve right away.

Roasted Cauliflower Tartine
with Dill Cashew Crema

A *tartine* is a French-style open-faced sandwich. Something about tartines has always fascinated me. This recipe takes a healthier twist by swapping out the bread for a roasted cauliflower steak. —*Mike* Serves 4

Roasted Cauliflower Tartine

1 medium head cauliflower, sliced lengthwise, keeping the core intact, into ½-inch-thick steaks (you should be able to get 4 to 6 good slices)

Extra-virgin olive oil

Pink Himalayan salt

Freshly ground black pepper

4 eggs

2 avocados, thinly sliced

1 large heirloom tomato, thinly sliced

1 (4-ounce) package smoked salmon

2 small radishes, sliced

½ teaspoon red pepper flakes (optional)

Fresh micro kale, for garnish

Coarse sea salt

Dill Cashew Crema

1 cup raw cashews

1 small clove garlic

¼ cup chopped fresh dill

½ teaspoon fresh lemon juice

1 Preheat the oven to 400°F.

2 Place the cauliflower steaks in a single layer on a baking sheet. Drizzle them with olive oil and season with salt and pepper. Roast for 40 minutes, until they are golden brown and fork-tender. Remove the cauliflower steaks from the baking sheet and set them aside on individual serving plates or on a platter.

3 While the cauliflower is roasting, bring a large saucepan of water to a boil. Gently add the eggs, reduce the heat to a simmer, and cook for 13 minutes. Drain, and set them aside to let cool slightly. Once they have cooled, peel the eggs and thinly slice them.

4 **To make the dill cashew crema:** Place the cashews in a high-powered blender, add ½ cup of water, and add the garlic, dill, lemon juice, ½ teaspoon salt, and ¼ teaspoon pepper. Blend on high speed until the dill cashew crema is completely smooth.

5 To build the tartines, spread each cauliflower steak with dill cashew crema followed by a layer of avocado slices and then a layer of tomato slices. Next, add the slices of smoked salmon and top them with the sliced eggs and radishes. Sprinkle with red pepper flakes (if using).

6 Garnish each tartine with micro kale, a few pinches of coarse sea salt, a drizzle of olive oil, and a couple grinds of fresh pepper.

Heirloom Tomatoes Stuffed with Crab

Lump crabmeat and tomatoes make for a perfect light lunch, which even in the fall, I like from time to time. I'm a major seafood lover and my daughter, Saylor, is the ultimate tomato girl (they've been her favorite food since she started eating), so this dish is for the girls in my house! Choose this to serve when you have guests coming over, as it's sure to impress. Since tomatoes aren't in season during the winter, once the leaves start falling, I try to make this salad as often as possible before I say good-bye to tomatoes for a bit. **Serves 2**

4 medium heirloom tomatoes

½ tablespoon Dijon mustard

½ tablespoon vegan mayo

½ teaspoon hot sauce

⅛ teaspoon garlic powder

3 scallions, white and green parts thinly sliced

½ tablespoon chopped fresh chives

1 tablespoon chopped fresh tarragon

2 tablespoons finely chopped celery

1 teaspoon grated lemon zest

½ tablespoon fresh lemon juice

1½ tablespoons plus 1 teaspoon extra-virgin olive oil

Pink Himalayan salt

Freshly ground black pepper

1 pound jumbo lump crabmeat

2 tablespoons celery leaves, for garnish

½ avocado, sliced

1 Slice the tops off the heirloom tomatoes and gently scoop out the core and seeds with a spoon. Set the tomato shells aside face down to drain the excess liquid.

2 In a large mixing bowl, combine the mustard, mayo, hot sauce, garlic powder, scallions, chives, tarragon, celery, lemon zest and juice, the 1½ tablespoons olive oil, and a couple big pinches each of salt and pepper. Whisk until well combined.

3 Place the crabmeat in a strainer to remove any extra liquid. Using your fingers, pick through the crab and remove any small pieces of shell that might have been left behind. Add the crabmeat to the dressing and fold to combine.

4 Fill each tomato evenly with the crab mixture. Top with a couple of celery leaves and avocado slices, and drizzle the remaining 1 teaspoon olive oil over the tomatoes. This can be served right away or chilled covered in the fridge to serve later.

Nashville Hot Chicken Salad Cups

On one of my first trips to Nashville, I tasted their famous hot chicken—and damn, even the mild version blew my socks off. Nashville's hot chicken is no joke, and it's become a must-do for people who are visiting from all around the country. Every spice-loving person comes saying they'll be able to handle it, but I've never heard one story of anyone being able to put it down without sweat dripping down their face and their insides burning! Insane! This version isn't nearly as hot, but it still has a good kick and it's one I make often. Traditional Nashville hot chicken doesn't come on a salad, but I like throwing it on some greens for extra nutrients. **Serves 4**

Chicken

2 cups oat flour

4 teaspoons garlic powder

4 teaspoons dried thyme

4 teaspoons paprika

4 teaspoons onion powder

1 tablespoon plus ½ teaspoon pink Himalayan salt

4 eggs

1 (5-ounce) bag tortilla chips (I like the Siete brand salted), crushed

1½ pounds skinless, boneless chicken breasts, cut into ¼-inch-thick strips

Avocado oil, for frying

Dressing

½ cup vegan mayo

⅓ cup goat's-milk yogurt

1 teaspoon champagne vinegar

3 tablespoons hot sauce, such as Frank's Red Hot

½ tablespoon extra-virgin olive oil

½ teaspoon chili powder

1 tablespoon cayenne pepper

¼ teaspoon garlic powder

½ teaspoon smoked paprika

½ teaspoon pink Himalayan salt

Salad Cups

1 medium head Bibb lettuce, leaves pulled apart

4 medium dill pickles, sliced

½ cup sliced cherry tomatoes

1 large avocado, sliced

(recipe continues)

1   **To make the hot chicken:** Set up an assembly station with 3 medium bowls. In the first bowl, combine ¾ cup of the oat flour, 2 teaspoons each of the garlic powder, thyme, paprika, and onion powder, and the 1 tablespoon salt; mix well. In the second bowl, whisk together the eggs. In the third bowl, combine the crushed chips, remaining 1¼ cups oat flour, remaining 2 teaspoons each of garlic powder, thyme, paprika, and onion powder, and remaining ½ teaspoon salt; mix well.

2   Take a chicken strip and coat it first in the flour mixture, then in the egg, then in the chip mixture, making sure to wipe off any excess coating after each bowl. Place the coated strip on a baking sheet or plate and set aside. Repeat with the remaining chicken strips.

3   Heat a large skillet over medium-high heat and fill with avocado oil until it is ½-inch deep. Once the oil is hot, add a few chicken strips in a single layer, making sure to avoid crowding the pan; you want the pieces close but not touching. Using tongs, move them around slightly so they don't burn. Fry until they are golden brown, 2 to 3 minutes on each side. Remove the cooked chicken and let it cool on a paper towel. Repeat with the remaining chicken strips, adding more oil needed.

4   Use an instant-read thermometer to see if the chicken is cooked (it should register 165°F on a few strips). If chicken isn't cooked all the way through, place the strips on a baking sheet and finish cooking them in a 350°F oven for 10 minutes.

5   **To make the dressing:** In a small bowl, combine the mayo, yogurt, champagne vinegar, hot sauce, olive oil, chili powder, cayenne pepper, garlic powder, smoked paprika, and salt. Stir well.

6   **To assemble the hot chicken salad cups:** Arrange the leaves of Bibb lettuce on a platter and fill each one with the fried chicken, slices of pickle, cherry tomatoes, and avocado. Liberally drizzle the hot dressing over each lettuce cup.

Tortilla-Crusted Chicken Fingers

I'm perfectly fine admitting that I like these chicken fingers just as much as my kids do. I make a big batch and throw some in the freezer to have on hand for school lunches. Serve them with homemade ranch dressing (page 263) and veggies for a kid-approved, and adult-appreciated, lunch. **Serves 6**

2 cups oat flour

4 teaspoons garlic powder

4 teaspoons dried thyme

4 teaspoons paprika

4 teaspoons onion powder

1 tablespoon plus ½ teaspoon pink Himalayan salt

4 eggs

1 (5-ounce) bag tortilla chips, crushed (I like the Siete brand salted)

1½ pounds skinless, boneless chicken breasts (about 2 large breasts), cut into ¼-inch thick strips

Avocado oil, for frying

1   Set up an assembly station with 3 medium bowls. In the first bowl, combine ¾ cup of the oat flour, 2 teaspoons each of the garlic powder, thyme, paprika, and onion powder, and 1 tablespoon salt; mix well. In the second bowl, whisk together the eggs. In the third bowl, combine the crushed chips, remaining 1¼ cups oat flour, remaining 2 teaspoons each of garlic powder, thyme, paprika, and onion powder, and the ½ teaspoon salt; stir to combine.

2   Take a chicken strip and coat it first in the flour mixture, then in the egg, then in the chip mixture, making sure to wipe off any excess coating after each bowl. Place the coated strip on a baking sheet or plate and set aside. Repeat with the remaining chicken strips.

3   Heat a large skillet over medium-high heat and fill with avocado oil until it is ½-inch full. Once the oil is hot, add a few chicken strips in a single layer, making sure to avoid crowding the pan; you want the pieces close but not touching. Using tongs, move them around slightly so they don't burn. Fry until they are golden brown, 2 to 3 minutes on each side. Remove the cooked strips and let them cool on a paper towel. Repeat with the remaining chicken strips and add more oil if needed.

4   Use an instant-read thermometer to see if the chicken is cooked (it should register 165°F on a few strips). If chicken isn't cooked all the way through, place the strips on a baking sheet and finish cooking them in a 350°F oven for 10 minutes.

Cucumber Salad
with Dill and Shallots

This salad is made up of my favorite fresh ingredients—
cucumbers, dill, and shallots—smothered in a creamy dressing.
I can eat the entire thing for a light lunch, but it also works
well as a side salad. **Serves 1 as a main salad or 2 to 3 as a side salad**

3 cups thinly sliced peeled
cucumbers

½ cup thinly sliced shallots

½ teaspoon pink Himalayan salt

⅓ cup vegan mayo

1 teaspoon champagne vinegar

½ teaspoon grated lemon zest

⅛ teaspoon red pepper flakes

2 tablespoons chopped fresh dill

½ tablespoon chopped fresh basil

¼ teaspoon freshly ground black
pepper

1 Place the cucumbers in a large mixing bowl and add the shallots. Sprinkle the salt evenly over the shallots and cucumber and let them sit for 5 to 10 minutes to pull out the excess moisture.

2 Meanwhile, in another large mixing bowl, combine the mayo, vinegar, lemon zest, red pepper flakes, dill, basil, and black pepper and whisk until well combined. Set the dressing aside.

3 Drain the liquid from the cucumber and shallots. Add them to the bowl of dressing, folding to combine. Serve right away or chill in the fridge for at least 30 minutes to make it more refreshing—the choice is yours and I actually like it both ways.

Chile Sesame Noodles
with Spicy Meatballs

Bison is one of my favorite proteins because it's lean and incredibly flavorful. Soba noodles won't spike blood sugar, and the spice in this dish gives it just the right kick. My kids won't eat spicy food yet, but this dish is heaven to me so it's the one time I'll make separate meals. I usually just make a batch of noodles and meatballs without the red pepper flakes and Sriracha for the kids. There are always leftovers, perfect to take to the office for lunch the next day.

If you haven't heard of tamari, it's made from fermented soybeans and has a flavor like soy sauce but is gluten-free and slightly better for you since it's higher in protein and contains antioxidants. It's my dad's secret ingredient in all his meatballs! **Serves 2**

Meatballs

1 pound ground bison

¼ cup almond flour

1 egg

2 cloves garlic, minced

½ tablespoon red pepper flakes

1 tablespoon Sriracha or your favorite hot sauce

3 tablespoons tamari

1 tablespoon grated fresh ginger

1 tablespoon chopped fresh parsley

2 teaspoons toasted sesame oil

Pink Himalayan salt

Freshly ground black pepper

Noodles

1 (8-ounce) package soba noodles

Sauce

¼ cup ponzu sauce

2 tablespoons rice vinegar

2 tablespoons raw honey

1 tablespoon grated fresh ginger

1 teaspoon chopped fresh Thai chile (jalapeño also works well)

1 tablespoon mirin

2 teaspoons toasted sesame oil

1 scallion, white and green parts sliced

1 clove garlic, minced

Garnish

2 scallions, white and green parts sliced

Sesame seeds

Sliced Thai chile

(recipe continues)

1 **Make the meatballs:** Preheat the oven to 375°F. Line a baking sheet with parchment paper; set aside.

2 In a large bowl, combine the bison, almond flour, egg, garlic, red pepper flakes, Sriracha, tamari, ginger, parsley, sesame oil, and a couple big pinches each of salt and pepper. Using your hands, mix together until combined. Roll the mixture into tablespoon-sized meatballs, and place them on the prepared baking sheet. Bake for 15 to 20 minutes, until cooked through.

3 **Meanwhile, prepare the noodles:** Bring a large pot of water to a boil, and cook the soba noodles according to the package directions. Drain, and rinse the noodles with cold water; set aside.

4 **Make the sauce:** In a small saucepan, combine the ponzu, rice vinegar, honey, ginger, Thai chile, mirin, sesame oil, scallion, and garlic. Bring to a simmer over medium-high heat and cook for 2 to 3 minutes, until well combined and fragrant. Remove from the heat and let cool.

5 Place the noodles in a large bowl and toss them with the sauce until they are coated. Evenly distribute the noodles among 2 bowls. Add a few meatballs to each bowl and garnish with the sliced scallions, sesame seeds, and sliced chile.

Burrito Bowls with Lime Rice

Mexican food is a staple in my house, so no matter what, burrito bowls are always a great choice. The key here is this flavorful chicken: I use all the regular spices, such as chili powder and cumin, but smoked paprika brings in another dimension that will have your taste buds thanking you. For the best results, let the chicken marinate at least an hour, but preferably overnight. **Serves 4**

2 pounds skinless, boneless chicken thighs

½ cup goat's-milk yogurt

1½ teaspoons chili powder

1½ teaspoons ground cumin

1 teaspoon smoked paprika

4 cloves garlic, minced

2 teaspoons grated lime zest

1½ teaspoons pink Himalayan salt

Freshly ground black pepper

2 cups Lime Rice (recipe follows)

1½ cups Simple Guacamole (page 245)

1½ cups Black "Refried" Beans (page 247)

1½ cups Roasted Salsa (page 246)

1½ cups Avocado Crema (page 245)

1 Place the chicken in a large ziplock bag or a baking dish. In a small bowl, combine the yogurt, chili powder, cumin, smoked paprika, garlic, lime zest, salt, and a pinch of pepper; whisk together. Pour the sauce over the chicken, massaging it into the meat. Place the bag (sealed) or baking dish (covered) in the fridge and chill for at least 1 hour or up to overnight.

2 When you're ready to cook the chicken, warm either a grill or a grill pan over medium heat. Cook the chicken for 3 minutes on each side until it is cooked through (it should register 165°F on an instant-read thermometer). Chop the chicken and set it aside.

3 To build the burrito bowls, spoon ½ cup of the Lime Rice into each of 4 bowls. Divide the chicken, guacamole, beans, salsa, and avocado crema among the bowls, and serve.

LIME RICE

Makes 2 cups

1 cup short-grain brown rice
4 tablespoons extra-virgin olive oil
1½ tablespoons fresh lime juice
1 teaspoon grated lime zest
1 teaspoon coarse sea salt

1 Cook the rice according to the package directions, adding 2 tablespoons of the olive oil to the cooking water.

2 In a large bowl, combine the cooked rice, lime juice and zest, salt, and the remaining 2 tablespoons olive oil.

Sunday Wings Two Ways

Football Sundays have always been a big day at my house. I like to make two types of wings for my family: My kids love the sweet sesame wings since they're coated in honey, and I typically go for the buffalo wings since I love the traditional flavor and a good kick. **Serves 4**

SWEET SESAME WINGS

2 pounds chicken wings
Pink Himalayan salt
Freshly ground black pepper
1 tablespoon virgin coconut oil
2 cloves garlic, minced
¼ cup coconut aminos
3 tablespoons raw honey
1 teaspoon sesame oil

1 Preheat the oven to 400°F.

2 Season the wings with salt and pepper. Place the wings on a wire rack on a rimmed baking sheet and bake until crispy, 40 minutes.

3 Meanwhile, in a small saucepan set over medium heat, cook the coconut oil and garlic together until aromatic, about 3 minutes. Add the coconut aminos, honey, and sesame oil and whisk until combined. Bring to a boil, then reduce to a simmer and cook, whisking occasionally, until the mixture has reduced by a third, about 4 minutes. Remove from the heat.

4 Place the wings in a large mixing bowl, pour the sauce over them, and toss to coat. Serve while the wings are hot.

SPICY BUFFALO WINGS

2 pounds chicken wings
Pink Himalayan salt
Freshly ground black pepper
¼ cup virgin coconut oil
½ cup hot sauce such as Frank's Red Hot
1 tablespoon white wine vinegar
½ teaspoon garlic powder

1 Preheat the oven to 400°F.

2 Season the wings with salt and pepper. Place the wings on a wire rack on a rimmed baking sheet and bake until crispy, 40 minutes.

3 Meanwhile, in a small saucepan set over medium heat, whisk together the coconut oil, hot sauce, vinegar, and garlic powder. Cook for 2 minutes for the flavors to combine.

4 Place the wings in a large mixing bowl, pour the sauce over them, and toss to coat. Serve while the wings are hot.

Game Day
Sheet Pan Nachos

During the fall months, Sundays are my favorite day of the week. I love having friends over to watch the football games and share some snacks. These nachos are my go-to when hosting because they are the perfect finger food. You can throw whatever you want on these nachos—I've included what we love, but feel free to make them your own. **Serves 6**

2 (5-ounce) bags tortilla chips (I like the Siete brand salted)

2 cups Black "Refried" Beans (page 247)

2 pounds shredded Slow-Cooker Chicken Tacos meat (see page 85)

8 ounces goat's-milk cheddar cheese, grated

1 cup full-fat sour cream

1 cup Simple Guacamole (page 245)

½ cup Roasted Salsa (page 246)

¾ cup chopped jalapeños (optional)

1   Preheat the oven to 375°F.

2   On a large baking sheet, spread the chips out evenly. Next, spoon the black bean spread over the chips gently, avoiding breaking the chips as much as possible. Scatter the shredded chicken on top, followed by the grated cheese.

3   Bake the nachos until the cheese starts to melt, 15 minutes. Remove the baking sheet from the oven and spoon the sour cream, guacamole, and salsa over the top. Sprinkle the jalapeños on last (if using). Serve immediately.

Big Mac Salad

There's nothing I love more than a good old-fashioned burger once in a while. Since I don't want to extend my indulgence to the bun that often, I make this hearty salad burger, with all the fixings, in salad form. **Serves 4**

1 pound ground beef

1 teaspoon garlic powder

1 teaspoon Worcestershire sauce

Pink Himalayan salt

Freshly ground black pepper

½ cup vegan mayo or your own favorite mayo

1 teaspoon red wine vinegar

2 teaspoons yellow mustard

1 teaspoon ketchup

½ teaspoon paprika

1 teaspoon minced dill pickle, plus ½ cup sliced dill pickles

1 teaspoon minced white onion

2 romaine lettuce hearts, cut in half lengthwise

1 cup halved grape tomatoes

¼ medium red onion, thinly sliced

1 teaspoon sesame seeds, for garnish

1   In a medium skillet, combine the ground beef with the garlic powder, Worcestershire sauce, and salt and pepper to taste. Cook over medium heat until the meat is browned and completely cooked through, 10 minutes. Set aside.

2   To make the "mac sauce," in a medium bowl, whisk together the mayo, vinegar, mustard, ketchup, paprika, minced pickle, white onion, and salt and pepper to taste. Set aside.

3   On a large plate, place a halved romaine heart. Assemble the salad in layers: First add the ground beef, followed by the tomatoes, sliced pickles, and red onion. Drizzle the "mac sauce" over the top and garnish with the sesame seeds. Repeat with the other romaine hearts.

Chopped Kale Caesar

Some people might not find salads to be comforting, but I would argue that a good Caesar salad absolutely checks that comfort box. Even in the colder months, I enjoy salads for lunch or as a side with dinner, and this one is hard to beat. Add grilled chicken or salmon for main-dish protein. **Serves 2 (makes 1 cup dressing)**

Dressing
5 medium cloves garlic, minced
1 tablespoon Dijon mustard
1 tablespoon champagne vinegar
Pink Himalayan salt
Freshly ground black pepper

2 tablespoons vegan mayo (or your own favorite mayo)
½ cup extra-virgin olive oil
Juice of ½ lemon
4 small oil-packed anchovies, minced

Salad
2 bunches Lacinato kale, finely chopped
1 avocado, diced
2 tablespoons pine nuts

1 **Prepare the dressing:** In a medium bowl, whisk together the garlic, mustard, and vinegar. Add a big pinch of salt and a pinch of pepper. Add the mayo, olive oil, lemon juice, and anchovies; stir to combine. Season with salt and pepper to taste. Store leftover dressing in an airtight container in the fridge up to 7 days.

2 **Make the salad:** Place the kale in a large bowl. Pour dressing to taste over the kale (you probably won't use all of it); toss to combine.

3 To serve, divide the kale between 2 plates. Add half of the diced avocado to each salad, followed by the pine nuts.

Roasted Eggplant

with Spiced Puree and Blistered Tomatoes

A picture of a dish I saw on social media inspired me to create this recipe with Mike. The spiced almond puree with cumin and chili powder brings in many elements of flavor. This is great for a savory lunch that isn't heavy or too complicated. **Serves 4**

1½ cups raw Marcona almonds

1 teaspoon fresh lemon juice

¼ cup plus 3 teaspoons avocado oil

½ teaspoon ground cumin

½ teaspoon smoked paprika

½ teaspoon ground turmeric

½ teaspoon chili powder

⅛ teaspoon dried thyme

¼ teaspoon garlic powder

Pink Himalayan salt

1 large eggplant, sliced into ½-inch-thick rounds

Freshly ground black pepper

1 cup cherry tomatoes

1 teaspoon chopped fresh tarragon

1 teaspoon chopped fresh basil

1 teaspoon minced shallot

⅓ cup fresh micro kale, for garnish

1 Preheat the oven to 425°F.

2 In a high-powered blender or food processor, combine the almonds, lemon juice, 2 teaspoons of the avocado oil, 1 cup of water, and the cumin, smoked paprika, turmeric, chili powder, thyme, garlic powder, and ½ teaspoon salt. Blend on high speed until the mixture is a completely smooth puree; set aside.

3 Coat the eggplant slices with the ¼ cup avocado oil and season them with salt and pepper. Arrange the slices in a single layer on a baking sheet. Roast for 20 to 25 minutes, until they are soft and tender. Remove from the oven and set aside.

4 In a medium sauté pan, heat the remaining 1 teaspoon avocado oil over high heat. Once it is hot, add the cherry tomatoes, tarragon, basil, shallot, and a pinch each of salt and pepper. Sauté, stirring the entire time, until the tomatoes start to crack and blister, about 5 minutes. Remove from the heat.

5 To assemble, spoon a layer of the almond puree on each serving plate (reserving some of the puree) and arrange the roasted eggplant on top. Next, layer the blistered tomatoes on top of the eggplant. Add dollops of the remaining almond puree, and garnish with the micro kale.

Slow-Cooker Chicken Tacos

These tacos are in heavy rotation at my house. They're perfect for a busy day since you only need 10 minutes in the morning to put the ingredients into your slow cooker. Then come dinnertime, all you have to do is whip up the guacamole and dinner is served. **Serves 6**

Chicken

2 pounds skinless, boneless chicken thighs

1 teaspoon smoked paprika

2 teaspoons ground cumin

1½ teaspoons chili powder

1½ teaspoons pink Himalayan salt

4 cloves garlic, minced

2 tablespoons virgin coconut oil

Grated zest of 1 lime

Juice of ½ lime

Tacos

12 tortillas (I like the Siete brand almond flour or cassava/chia flour)

1 cup chopped romaine lettuce

1½ cups Simple Guacamole (page 245)

1½ cups Avocado Crema (page 245)

1 cup Black "Refried" Beans (page 247)

1 cup Roasted Salsa (page 246)

1 Set your slow cooker on low to cook for 8 hours, or on high to cook for 4 hours.

2 Place the chicken, smoked paprika, cumin, chili powder, salt, garlic, coconut oil, and lime zest and juice in the cooker and cover it. Cook, stirring the chicken every hour or so if possible (this is not necessary).

3 Once the chicken is tender (this will happen about 2 hours into your 8 hours on low or 4 hours on high), shred it, using 2 forks. Continue to cook for the remaining time on low or high, stirring it every hour or so.

4 Divide the chicken among the tortillas and top it with the lettuce, guacamole, avocado crema, black beans, and salsa.

Soups

White Chicken Chili with Salsa Verde

I like this white version of chili because it's lighter than the traditional hearty ones and still will knock your socks off with its perfect poblano kick. This recipe makes a big batch, so eat it for a few days running or freeze some to enjoy later. To defrost the frozen chili, I simply leave the container in my kitchen sink for a few hours before heating it up in a large saucepan. **Serves 8**

1 tablespoon avocado oil

2 pounds skinless, boneless chicken thighs, cut into ½-inch pieces

2 small poblano chiles, seeds removed, chopped

1 small white onion, chopped

1 jalapeño, seeds removed, diced

2 teaspoons chopped garlic

2 teaspoons ground cumin

1 teaspoon smoked paprika

½ teaspoon dried oregano

¼ teaspoon garlic powder

¼ teaspoon freshly ground black pepper

¼ teaspoon onion powder

Pink Himalayan salt

2 (4-ounce) cans chopped green chiles

1 cup jarred salsa verde

2 (19-ounce) cans cannellini beans, drained and rinsed

4 cups chicken stock

Juice of 1 lime

1 avocado, diced, for garnish

1 cup Cashew Crema (page 259), for garnish

1   In a large Dutch oven set over medium-high heat, add the avocado oil. Add the chicken and cook until the chicken pieces are browned, 15 minutes. Add the poblanos, onion, and jalapeño, and continue cooking until the onion has softened, about 10 minutes.

2   Add the garlic, cumin, paprika, oregano, garlic powder, pepper, onion powder, and a big pinch of salt. Stir, and cook for 10 minutes, until fragrant. Reduce the heat to low and add the green chiles, salsa verde, and cannellini beans; cook for 15 minutes, stirring it occasionally to bring the flavors together.

3   Bring the heat back up to medium and add the chicken stock and lime juice. Bring the chili to a simmer and let it cook, occasionally stirring it from the bottom to prevent burning, for 1 hour and 15 minutes, until thickened. Add more salt and pepper as needed.

4   Garnish each bowl of chili with diced avocado and a dollop of the Cashew Crema.

Ground Bison Slow-Cooker Chili

To me, slow-cooker chili is one of those all-time comfort food classics. It may be my Midwest roots, but that chili was always a staple at Halloween or block parties when I was growing up, and I continue that tradition every Halloween today. Bison is lean and full of flavor, and this recipe is a great alternative to a traditional beef chili. This is a perfect dish to prep ahead of time and then let cook all day in the slow cooker. —*Mike* Serves 8

1 tablespoon extra-virgin olive oil

1 large sweet onion, chopped

1 green bell pepper, chopped

3 cloves garlic, minced

2 pounds ground bison

2 (14.5-ounce) cans diced fire-roasted tomatoes, drained

1 (7-ounce) can tomato paste

1 cup beef stock

1 tablespoon Worcestershire sauce

1 tablespoon chili powder

2 teaspoons ground cumin

2 teaspoons paprika

½ teaspoon ground coriander

Pink Himalayan salt

Freshly ground black pepper

1 (15-ounce) can red kidney beans, drained and rinsed

1 (15-ounce) can pinto beans, drained and rinsed

2 scallions, white and green parts chopped, for garnish

1 Turn your slow cooker to the low setting.

2 Heat the olive oil in a large skillet over medium heat. Add the onion and bell pepper, and sauté for 5 minutes. Add the garlic and sauté for an additional minute, until fragrant. Transfer the onion/pepper mixture to the slow cooker.

3 Return the skillet to medium-high heat. Add the bison and cook, stirring occasionally, until it is browned, 5 minutes. Add the bison to the slow cooker.

4 Stir the fire-roasted tomatoes, tomato paste, beef stock, Worcestershire sauce, chili powder, cumin, paprika, and coriander into the mixture in the slow cooker. Season with salt and pepper. Cover the slow cooker and cook on the low setting for 4 hours.

5 Add both beans to the mixture in the slow cooker and stir to combine. Let the chili cook, still on the low setting, for 1 more hour.

6 To serve, spoon the chili into serving bowls and garnish with the scallions.

Butternut Squash and Leek Chowder with Smoked Salmon

There's something about the sweet butternut squash and the subtlety of the smoked salmon that really pairs well. This is a soup that you can serve at a dinner party or just because. It's super-rich and comforting, but if you aren't a fish fan, no problem, leave it out—this soup is great on its own as well. —*Mike* Serves 6

1½ tablespoons avocado oil, plus more for the baking sheet

2 medium butternut squash

3 medium leeks, cleaned and diced

1 jalapeño, seeds removed, minced (optional)

2 carrots, diced

1 medium shallot, coarsely chopped

1 teaspoon paprika

1 teaspoon dried thyme

2 teaspoons chopped fresh sage

½ teaspoon ground turmeric

¼ teaspoon ground nutmeg

Pink Himalayan salt

5 cups chicken stock

⅓ cup coconut cream

½ teaspoon champagne vinegar

1 pound smoked salmon, chopped or ripped into ½-inch pieces

Freshly ground black pepper

½ tablespoon chopped fresh chives, for garnish

1   Preheat the oven to 350°F. Grease a large baking sheet with avocado oil.

2   Slice the butternut squash in half lengthwise and scoop out the seeds. Lay the halves face-down on the prepared baking sheet and bake until tender, 35 minutes. Scoop the cooked squash out of the shells and set it aside in a bowl.

3   Heat the avocado oil in a large saucepan over medium-high heat. Add the leeks, jalapeño (if using), carrots, and shallot. Sauté for 15 minutes, until tender. Add the paprika, thyme, sage, turmeric, nutmeg, and a pinch of salt. Raise the heat to high and sauté for an additional 5 minutes. Then add the cooked butternut squash, chicken stock, coconut cream, and champagne vinegar; stir until fully combined. Bring the soup to a simmer and let it cook for 20 minutes, stirring it often. Add salt to taste.

4   Working in batches, transfer the soup to a high-powered blender and blend on high speed until it is smooth. Only fill the blender up about half way to avoid it spilling and burning your hands.

5   To serve, place ¼ cup of the smoked salmon in each serving bowl, and ladle the hot soup over it. Garnish with pepper, a sprinkling of chives, and the remaining salmon.

Chicken Tortilla Soup
with Poached Eggs

I've loved traditional tortilla soup for years, but after a trip to Mexico where I had it with poached eggs, I will never have it another way ever again; eggs pair perfectly with the rich flavors of the soup. I like my poached eggs a little runny, but feel free to cook yours until the yolk is cooked through. And if you've never made poached eggs, just make sure to get your water going like a whirlpool before slipping the eggs in. **Serves 4**

2 tablespoons avocado oil

1 medium yellow onion, diced

2 medium poblano chiles, seeds removed, diced

2 jalapeños , seeds removed, diced

4 cloves garlic, minced

2 (14.5-ounce) cans diced fire-roasted tomatoes, drained

1 tablespoon chili powder

2 teaspoons ground cumin

1 teaspoon smoked paprika

4 cups (2 quarts) chicken stock

4 tortillas (I like the Siete brand almond flour, but feel free to use your favorite), toasted

4 cups chopped cooked chicken

1 (14.5-ounce) can black beans, drained and rinsed

Grated zest and juice of 1 lime

Pink Himalayan salt

Freshly ground black pepper

8 eggs

White wine vinegar

1 avocado, sliced

¼ cup chopped fresh cilantro

4 scallions, white and green parts sliced

1 lime, cut into 8 wedges

1 In a medium Dutch oven set over medium heat, warm the avocado oil. Add the onion, poblanos, jalapeños, and garlic. Sauté until the onion is translucent, 10 minutes. Add the fire-roasted tomatoes, chili powder, cumin, and paprika, and cook for another 10 minutes.

2 Add the chicken stock and bring to a simmer.

3 Transfer half of the soup mixture to a blender, and add the toasted tortillas by breaking them up using your hands. Blend on high speed until completely smooth. Return the mixture to the Dutch oven and continue cooking over medium heat until it thickens slightly, 20 minutes.

(recipe continues)

4   Reduce the heat to low and add the cooked chicken, black beans, and lime zest and juice. Season with salt and pepper to taste and cook for 20 minutes to allow everything to come together.

5   Meanwhile, poach the eggs: Fill a large saucepan halfway with water and warm it over medium heat. Crack each egg into an individual ramekin or small bowl. Add a pinch of salt and a dash of vinegar to the hot water. With a spoon, stir the water until you've created a tornado motion. Slip the eggs, one at a time, into the swirling water, and cook until the eggs are completely white but you can still see a little yellow of the yolk, 4 minutes. Remove the poached eggs from the water with a slotted spoon and pat dry. Season with salt and pepper.

6   To assemble the soup, place 2 poached eggs in each serving bowl. Ladle the soup over the eggs and garnish each bowl with the avocado, cilantro, and scallions and serve each bowl with 2 lime wedges.

Classic Tomato Soup

There's something so comforting about a big bowl of tomato soup. I like it best with a grilled (goat) cheese sandwich or with shredded goat's-milk cheddar sprinkled on top, but I've left those dairy counterparts out of the recipe here for those of you avoiding dairy altogether. **Serves 6**

2 tablespoons extra-virgin olive oil, plus more for garnish

1 small onion, diced

2 medium cloves garlic, minced

2 (28-ounce) cans peeled tomatoes, with their juice

4 cups Chicken Bone Broth, homemade (page 99) or your favorite chicken stock

4 tablespoons chopped fresh basil

⅓ cup coconut cream

1 teaspoon coconut sugar

Pink Himalayan salt

Freshly ground black pepper

1　In a large saucepan, heat the olive oil over medium heat. Add the onion and garlic. Sauté together until the onion is translucent, 10 minutes. Add the tomatoes, with their juice, and the Chicken Bone Broth. Bring to a simmer and cook for 10 minutes.

2　Transfer the mixture to a high-powered blender, add 2 tablespoons of the basil, and puree until completely smooth. Return the puree to the saucepan and bring to a simmer. Add the coconut cream, coconut sugar, and salt and pepper to taste. Continue to cook for 15 to 20 minutes for the flavors to combine.

3　Garnish each serving with a drizzle of olive oil and the remaining 2 tablespoons basil.

Bone Broth Chicken Noodle Soup

Known for helping to reduce inflammation, bone broth is also great for the immune system and alleviates the common cold. Now, chicken noodle (bone broth) soup really can be just what the doctor ordered. Luckily my kids also love this, maybe because they know it will help them feel better when they're under the weather. **Serves 8**

3 skinless, boneless chicken breasts

Pink Himalayan salt

1 teaspoon freshly ground black pepper, plus more to taste

2 tablespoons avocado oil

1 cup chopped red onion

1 cup chopped celery

½ cup chopped leeks

1 cup chopped carrots

2 cloves garlic, minced

12 cups (3 quarts) Chicken Bone Broth (recipe follows)

1 tablespoon chopped fresh basil

1 tablespoon chopped fresh parsley

1 tablespoon chopped fresh thyme

2 bay leaves

2 cups brown rice pasta shells

1 teaspoon champagne vinegar

1   Preheat the oven to 425°F.

2   Season the chicken with salt to taste and the pepper, place it on a baking sheet, and roast for 25 minutes. Remove it from the oven and let it cool slightly before cutting it into small cubes.

3   In a large pot set over medium heat, heat the avocado oil. Add the red onion, celery, leeks, carrots, garlic, and 2 teaspoons salt. Sauté the vegetables until they are tender, 10 minutes. Add the cubed cooked chicken, bone broth, basil, parsley, thyme, and bay leaves and bring to a simmer. Continue cooking for 30 minutes.

4   Once all the flavors have combined, add the pasta and reduce the heat to medium-low. Once the noodles are soft, add the champagne vinegar and black pepper to taste. Remove bay leaves and discard. Serve hot.

CHICKEN BONE BROTH

Makes 12 cups (the exact amount for the chicken noodle soup)

2 pounds chicken bones

½ tablespoon fresh lemon juice

1 small white onion, coarsely chopped

3 medium carrots, coarsely chopped

3 stalks celery, coarsely chopped

2 cloves garlic

1 cup Italian parsley leaves and stems

1 large bay leaf

6 sprigs fresh thyme

1 tablespoon pink Himalayan salt

1 teaspoon black peppercorns

In the colder months, I like to occasionally start my morning with a cup of bone broth to keep the common cold at bay. Save the bones from a roasted chicken or get raw bones from your local butcher for this recipe.

1 Preheat the oven to 400°F.

2 Place the chicken bones in a roasting pan and roast until they are golden brown, 35 minutes. Transfer the roasted bones to a large stockpot.

3 Pour 16 cups (4 quarts) cold water and the lemon juice over the bones and let sit for 10 minutes. Then turn the heat under the pot to medium-high and slowly bring the liquid to a boil. Then reduce it to a simmer.

4 Add the onion, carrots, celery, garlic, parsley, bay leaf, thyme sprigs, salt, and peppercorns and stir to combine. Continue to simmer for 12 to 24 hours, making sure not to let the liquid reach a vigorous boil at any point.

5 The broth will be done when the bones eventually start to crumble (when all their nutrients and proteins have been extracted). Once you see this happening with the majority of your bones, remove the pot from the heat and let the broth cool slightly.

6 Using a metal strainer or a fine colander, strain the bone broth into a container to remove all of the bones and vegetables. Let the strained broth cool completely, then use it right away or store it in airtight containers in the fridge.

Cozy
Nights

Eggplant Parmesan

This recipe hits close to home for me. I can remember coming home after playing in the neighborhood on a cold fall day and finding this on the kitchen table. This is a lightened-up version of my mom's, since here we bake the eggplant instead of frying it, but the dish doesn't skip a beat on the flavor. It's just as amazing as when I was a kid and it brings back so many comforting memories. —*Mike* Serves 6

2 teaspoons extra-virgin olive oil

3 eggs

1 cup gluten-free bread crumbs

⅓ cup oat flour

½ cup freshly grated Manchego cheese

½ teaspoon dried basil

¼ teaspoon garlic powder

½ teaspoon pink Himalayan salt

½ teaspoon freshly ground black pepper

2 medium eggplants, peeled and sliced into ¼-inch-thick rounds

¼ cup chopped fresh basil

2½ cups Dad's Famous Pasta Sauce (page 255)

½ cup grated buffalo mozzarella

6 whole fresh basil leaves, for garnish

1 Preheat the oven to 400°F. Coat 2 baking sheets with olive oil. Set aside.

2 In a medium shallow dish, whisk the eggs with 3 tablespoons water until frothy. In another medium shallow dish, combine the bread crumbs, oat flour, ¼ cup of the Manchego, the dried basil, garlic powder, salt, and pepper. Mix together well. Dip the eggplant slices into the egg mixture, coat them with the bread-crumb mixture, and then place them in a single layer on the prepared baking sheets.

3 Bake the eggplant for 15 minutes. Then turn the slices over and bake for an additional 15 minutes, until crisp and golden. Remove from the oven and set aside. Leave the oven on.

4 In a medium mixing bowl, mix the chopped fresh basil with the pasta sauce. Spread ½ cup of the sauce on the bottom of a 9 × 13-inch baking dish. Arrange half of the eggplant slices over the sauce, overlapping them slightly. Spoon 1 cup of the sauce over the eggplant, and sprinkle ¼ cup of the mozzarella over that. Add another layer of eggplant slices and top with the remaining sauce. Sprinkle with the remaining ¼ cup mozzarella and remaining ¼ cup Manchego.

5 Bake, uncovered, until the sauce is bubbly and the top is golden brown, 15 minutes. Let the dish cool for 10 minutes before slicing and serving. Garnish each serving with a fresh basil leaf.

Alfredo Cauliflower Casserole

This casserole hits the spot on a cold winter night when all I want to do is cuddle up with my kids on the couch and watch a movie. It's creamy without using dairy, and the caramelized leeks give a delicate crunch for the ultimate savory dish. **Serves 6**

1 large head cauliflower, core removed and finely chopped in a food processor

3 tablespoons virgin coconut oil

1 clove garlic, minced

2 tablespoons arrowroot powder

2½ cups almond milk

1½ teaspoons pink Himalayan salt

¼ teaspoon freshly ground black pepper

2 tablespoons chopped fresh chives

1 tablespoon avocado oil

1½ pounds skinless, boneless chicken thighs, cut into bite-sized pieces

1 cup chopped leeks

1   Preheat the oven to 350°F. Line an 8 × 11-inch baking dish with parchment paper.

2   Place the chopped cauliflower in the prepared baking dish and set it aside.

3   In a large saucepan, melt the coconut oil over medium heat. Add the garlic and cook for 2 minutes, until aromatic. In a small bowl, whisk the arrowroot powder with 2 tablespoons of water. Add the dissolved arrowroot to the oil and garlic, whisking continuously to prevent clumping. Add the almond milk and whisk until the sauce is smooth and has thickened, 4 minutes. Add ½ teaspoon of the salt, the pepper, and the chives and stir to combine. Pour the sauce into a medium bowl and set it aside.

4   Heat the avocado oil in the same saucepan over medium heat. Add the chicken pieces, season them with the remaining 1 teaspoon salt, and sauté for 5 minutes, until browned. Place the cooked chicken in the same baking dish as the cauliflower; toss to combine.

5   Pour the sauce into the baking dish until the chicken and cauliflower are completely covered, then sprinkle the leeks over the top. Bake, covered with foil, for 40 minutes. Then remove the foil and bake for another 15 minutes, until the leeks are golden brown. Serve hot.

Apple Butter Lamb Chops

Nothing screams "fall" quite like apple butter. If you aren't familiar with it, apple butter is a highly concentrated form of applesauce. Here, the sweet apples mix perfectly with the strong flavor of lamb: a match made in heaven. This dish goes well with roasted veggies and the mini Manchego and chive cauliflower biscuits on page 155. If you only have access to lamb chops and not a rack of lamb, no worries—just use the chops (I would get at least 8)! **Serves 4**

2 frenched racks of lamb (ask your butcher to cut the lamb this way)

1 teaspoon Dijon mustard

1 tablespoon chopped fresh rosemary

Pink Himalayan salt

Freshly ground black pepper

1 tablespoon extra-virgin olive oil

2 tablespoons apple cider vinegar

¼ cup apple butter

1 teaspoon chopped fresh chives

1 Preheat the oven to 375°F.

2 On a small baking sheet, rub the racks of lamb with the mustard, rosemary, ½ teaspoon salt, and ½ teaspoon pepper.

3 In a medium skillet set over high heat, warm ½ tablespoon of the olive oil. Sear the lamb on each side 3 minutes until browned. Remove the lamb from the heat and place it back on the baking sheet, bone-side down.

4 In a small bowl, mix the remaining ½ tablespoon olive oil with the apple cider vinegar, apple butter, and a pinch each of salt and pepper. Spread half of this mixture all over the racks of lamb. Roast for 20 to 25 minutes, until the meat is cooked medium-rare (145°F on an instant-read thermometer), or cook it to your liking. Let the meat rest for 15 minutes before slicing the racks into chops.

5 To serve, drizzle the remaining apple butter sauce over the chops, and garnish with the chives.

Squash Carbonara with Bacon and Peas

Carbonara is traditionally very rich, creamy, and decadent. But here we use butternut squash noodles, created with a spiralizer, so you won't need a nap after eating it. If you don't have a spiralizer or just want a slightly heavier dish that's closer to the classic version, you can use brown rice noodles or chickpea flour noodles. **Serves 4**

4 eggs

½ cup grated Manchego cheese

2 tablespoons extra-virgin olive oil

Pink Himalayan salt

Freshly ground black pepper

8 slices bacon, diced

⅓ cup chopped shallots

2 cloves garlic, minced

1 tablespoon coarsely chopped fresh sage

1 tablespoon chopped fresh basil

½ cup frozen English peas

1 medium butternut squash, spiralized

Chicken stock (optional)

1   In a small mixing bowl, whisk together the eggs, ¼ cup of the Manchego cheese, and 1 tablespoon of the olive oil until no egg whites are visible. Season with a pinch each of salt and pepper; set aside.

2   In a large skillet, heat the remaining 1 tablespoon olive oil over medium heat. Add the bacon and cook, stirring occasionally, until it is just crispy, 10 minutes. Use a slotted spoon to transfer the bacon to a paper towel.

3   Pour off half of the bacon fat left in the skillet, then add the shallots and garlic to the skillet. Season with salt and pepper. Cook over medium heat, stirring often, for 5 minutes.

Then reduce the heat to low and add the sage, basil, and English peas. Cook for 3 minutes. Return the bacon to the skillet and raise the heat to medium. Add the spiralized squash, stirring everything together. Reduce the heat to low and slowly poor the egg mixture into the skillet, stirring constantly so the eggs don't scramble. If this is done correctly, the sauce will have a nice velvety texture. You can add chicken stock, 1 teaspoon at a time, if needed to bring back the creaminess.

4   To serve, garnish the carbonara with the remaining ¼ cup Manchego and a pinch of black pepper.

Stuffed Shells with Cashew Ricotta

When we had stuffed shells growing up, it meant either it was Sunday supper or my parents were going out for the night, in which case my mom would throw a batch of her frozen shells into the oven. This version cuts out all of the cheese and subs in creamy cashews, but you surely won't miss the traditional dairy at all. This classic dish still delivers that Italian comfort-food feeling. I use Kristin's dad's sauce here to elevate it even more. —*Mike*

Serves 6

24 jumbo brown rice pasta shells

4 cups raw cashews

Juice of 2 lemons

Pink Himalayan salt

2 cups chopped fresh spinach

1 egg plus 1 egg yolk

½ cup chopped fresh basil

1 tablespoon dried oregano

3 cloves garlic, minced

3½ cups Dad's Famous Pasta Sauce (page 255)

1 tablespoon chopped fresh parsley, for garnish

1 Preheat the oven to 350°F.

2 Bring a large pot of salted water to a boil, and cook the brown rice shells according to the package directions. Drain and rinse them with cold water; set aside.

3 To make the cashew ricotta, place the cashews in a high-powered blender or a food processor and add 1 cup plus 2 tablespoons water. Add the lemon juice and 1 teaspoon salt. Blend on high speed until smooth, using a spatula to scrape down the sides of the blender as needed.

4 Place the cashew mixture in a medium bowl. Add the spinach, egg and egg yolk, basil, oregano, a pinch of salt, and the garlic. Stir together until well combined.

5 Spread half of the pasta sauce on the bottom of a 9 × 13-inch baking dish. Using a spoon, scoop the cashew ricotta mixture into each shell, then arrange the shells in the baking dish. Spoon the rest of the sauce over the filled shells. Cover the dish with foil and bake for 45 minutes.

6 Let the stuffed shells cool slightly before serving. To serve, sprinkle with the chopped parsley.

Butternut Squash Gnocchi

If I could choose my last meal on earth, it would be gnocchi. Maybe it's the Italian in me, or maybe it's because they are just plain good, but gnocchi will forever and always be my go-to comfort dish. I've "health-ified" them here, using gluten-free oat flour and adding butternut squash for vitamins and minerals. "Health-ified" or not, these satisfy my need for gnocchi every time. **Serves 4**

2 pounds butternut squash, peeled, seeded, and cut into cubes

4 cups oat flour, plus more for rolling

½ cup grated Manchego cheese, plus more for garnish

Pink Himalayan salt

Freshly ground black pepper

½ teaspoon dried thyme

1 egg

½ cup extra-virgin olive oil

4 cloves garlic, minced

3 teaspoons fresh lemon juice

6 fresh sage leaves, chopped

1 tablespoon chopped fresh parsley

1 Cover a large baking sheet with parchment paper and set it aside.

2 Bring a large pot of water to a boil. Add the squash cubes and cook they are until fork-tender, 10 to 15 minutes. Drain, then place the squash in a food processor. Pulse for 2 minutes or until completely smooth.

3 Return the squash to the (empty) pot and cook it over medium heat for 5 minutes, stirring occasionally. You should have about 2 cups of butternut squash puree. Remove from the heat and let it cool slightly.

4 In a large bowl, combine 2 cups of the oat flour with the Manchego cheese, 1 teaspoon salt, a pinch of pepper, and the thyme. Stir together. Make a well in the center of the dry ingredients, and add the egg and the squash puree to the well. Mix, using your hands, until just combined. Add the remaining 2 cups oat flour and mix until it barely sticks to your hands and resembles dough.

(recipe continues)

5 Dust a cutting board or other work surface with oat flour. Divide the gnocchi dough into 8 equal portions. Working with one portion at a time, roll the dough out into a ½-inch-thick rope; then cut the rope into ¾-inch-long pieces. Place the gnocchi on the prepared baking sheet and continue with the remaining dough. Set aside.

6 In a large sauté pan, cook the olive oil over medium heat for 5 minutes, stirring occasionally. Add the garlic, lemon juice, sage, and ½ teaspoon salt; cook for another 5 minutes. Reduce the heat to low to keep the oil mixture warm.

7 Bring a large pot of salted water to a boil. Gently place half of the gnocchi in the boiling water and cook until they rise to the top, 10 to 15 minutes. Remove the gnocchi with a slotted spoon, place them in the sauté pan, and fold them into the olive oil sauce, coating them completely. Repeat with the remaining gnocchi.

8 Garnish the gnocchi with the parsley and serve right away.

Creamy Garlic Halibut

I don't typically think of fish when I'm thinking of comfort food . . . unless it's smothered in a garlicky mayo. This dish has rich flavors, so pair it with something simple like roasted asparagus and a side salad for balance. **Serves 4**

2 pounds wild-caught halibut fillet

Pink Himalayan salt

Freshly ground black pepper

¼ cup vegan mayo

5 cloves garlic, minced

¼ cup goat's-milk butter or vegan butter, at room temperature

1 teaspoon onion powder

1 Preheat the oven to 450°F. Line a small baking sheet with foil.

2 Place the halibut on the prepared baking sheet and rub salt and pepper all over it. Bake 8 for 10 minutes, until cooked to medium (the center should be opaque).

3 Meanwhile, in a small bowl, mix the mayo, garlic, butter, and onion powder together until combined (this is your "dressing").

4 Spread the dressing over the halibut. Turn on the broiler and broil the halibut for 2 to 3 minutes, until the fish is a light golden brown. Enjoy immediately.

Salad Pizza with Cauliflower Crust

I like getting as many greens in as possible, even when eating pizza, so I throw a yummy salad on top here. The recipe replaces the traditional doughy pizza crust with a cauliflower one. This is loaded with veggies but still satisfies any pizza craving. This crust is a great base for just about any topping combo your heart desires. I like doubling—or even tripling—the recipe to make a bunch of pizzas to have for leftover lunch the next day as well. **Serves 2**

Crust

1 head cauliflower, cored and cut into medium pieces

½ cup almond flour

½ teaspoon dried basil

½ teaspoon pink Himalayan salt

½ teaspoon paprika

¼ teaspoon garlic powder

2 eggs

Toppings

1 tablespoon chopped roasted garlic (recipe follows)

½ cup shredded Manchego cheese

½ teaspoon red pepper flakes

¼ cup fresh basil leaves

4 cups loosely packed baby arugula

1½ tablespoons extra-virgin olive oil

¼ cup balsamic vinegar

Pink Himalayan salt

10 thin strips of prosciutto

1 Preheat the oven to 400°F. Line a large baking sheet with parchment paper.

2 **Make the crust:** Pulse the cauliflower pieces in a food processor until they resemble rice. In a large skillet, cook the cauliflower over medium heat, stirring constantly, for 15 minutes until golden brown. Let it cool slightly.

3 Place the cauliflower in a towel or in a fine-mesh sieve. Drain out the extra moisture by squeezing the towel over the sink or by pressing down on the cauliflower in the sieve.

4 In a medium mixing bowl, combine the cauliflower with the almond flour, basil, salt, paprika, garlic powder, and eggs, mixing to form a dough. Transfer the cauliflower dough to the center of the prepared baking sheet and spread it out into a round so it resembles a pizza crust. Bake for 15 minutes. Rotate the crust and bake for an additional 10 minutes, until slightly golden brown.

5 Sprinkle the roasted garlic, shredded Manchego, red pepper flakes, and basil leaves over the crust. Bake for another 10 minutes, until the cheese has melted.

6 While the pizza is baking, toss the arugula in a large bowl with the olive oil, balsamic, and a pinch of salt.

7 Remove the pizza from the oven and scatter the tossed arugula and the prosciutto strips over the top. Enjoy immediately. (I've also saved some in an airtight container and eaten it the next day.)

ROASTED GARLIC

Makes 1 bulb

1 bulb garlic
Extra-virgin olive oil

Roast the garlic: Preheat the oven to 400°F. Cut top off of head of garlic. Wrap the head of garlic in the foil and drizzle with olive oil. Fold tin foil so there is a little chimney spout. Roast for 35 minutes.

Chicken Ragu à la King

I think this is my favorite recipe in the whole book. In fact, it's one of my favorites ever. While I love to make this on a cold winter's night (when I'm cozy in sweats with my hair in a ponytail), it's also light enough to make on a warm summer night (and eat outside in jean shorts with a glass of chilled white wine). **Serves 6**

2 tablespoons extra-virgin olive oil

½ pound bacon, chopped

1½ pounds skin-on, bone-in chicken thighs

Pink Himalayan salt

Freshly ground black pepper

2 medium yellow onions, finely chopped

1 fennel bulb, thinly sliced

6 sprigs fresh thyme

½ cup dry white wine

½ cup full-fat coconut milk

1 cup frozen peas

¾ (16-ounce) package gluten-free pasta of your choice (I like brown rice penne)

1 Heat the olive oil in a large Dutch oven over medium heat, and cook the bacon until it is crispy, about 8 minutes. Remove the bacon from the pot and set it aside on a paper towel.

2 Season the chicken thighs with salt and pepper. Place them in the Dutch oven, skin-side down, and sauté until they are golden brown, 5 minutes. Flip them over and cook for 5 minutes on the second side. Transfer the chicken to a plate.

3 Add the onions and fennel to the pot and cook until they are soft, 8 minutes. Add the thyme sprigs and the white wine; cook until the wine has reduced by half, 6 minutes.

4 Return the chicken and the bacon to the Dutch oven and add enough water to barely cover the ingredients. Simmer with the lid ajar for 45 minutes.

5 Remove the chicken from the Dutch oven and let it cool slightly. Then use 2 forks to shred the chicken, discarding the skin and bones. Add the coconut milk to the pot and cook until it reduces slightly, 10 minutes. Place the shredded chicken and the peas in the pot, and season with salt and pepper.

6 Meanwhile, cook the pasta according to the package directions. Drain and rinse it, then add it to the chicken mixture in the Dutch oven. Cook until the flavors combine, 5 minutes. Remove thyme sprigs and serve immediately.

Red Wine–Braised Short Ribs

Short ribs will always be a favorite of mine for their fall-off-the-bone tenderness. Here red wine brings out the rich, bold flavors. I love this served over pureed cauliflower or parsnips, with the spicy braised kale on page 151 alongside. This is a hearty, cozy dinner, perfect for date night (there will be leftovers for lunch the next day!) or for a small dinner party. The short ribs cook for hours, so when your guests arrive, your house will smell amazing and everyone will be excited about what's to come. **Serves 6**

5 pounds bone-in beef short ribs (ask your butcher to cut them into 2-inch pieces)

Pink Himalayan salt

Freshly ground black pepper

3 tablespoons avocado oil

2 medium onions, coarsely chopped

3 medium carrots, coarsely chopped

2 celery stalks, coarsely chopped

3 tablespoons oat flour

1 tablespoon tomato paste

2 cups dry red wine (I like Cabernet Sauvignon)

8 sprigs fresh thyme

1 teaspoon dried oregano

2 sprigs fresh rosemary

2 bay leaves

1 garlic bulb, unpeeled, cut in half crosswise

4 cups beef stock

1/3 cup chopped fresh parsley

1 Season the short ribs heavily with salt and pepper. In a large Dutch oven, heat the avocado oil over medium-high heat. Working in 2 batches, brown the short ribs on all sides, 5 to 8 minutes per batch. As they are done, transfer the browned short ribs to a plate and set aside.

2 Add the onions, carrots, and celery to the same Dutch oven and cook over medium-high heat, stirring often, until the onions are browned, 5 minutes.

3 Add the oat flour and tomato paste, stirring constantly until they are well combined and everything is a deep red color, 3 to 5 minutes. Stir in the red wine.

4 Return the short ribs, along with any accumulated juice, to the Dutch oven and bring to a boil. Reduce the heat to medium and simmer until the wine is reduced by half, 20 to 25 minutes.

(recipe continues)

5   Meanwhile, preheat the oven to 350°F.

6   Add the thyme sprigs, oregano, rosemary sprigs, bay leaves, and garlic to the Dutch oven. Stir in the stock and bring everything to a boil. Cover, transfer the Dutch oven to the oven, and cook until the short ribs are tender, 3 hours.

7   Place the short ribs on a large platter. Strain the cooking liquid from the pot into a measuring cup. Remove the fat from the surface of the sauce and discard it. Season the sauce with salt and pepper to taste.

8   To serve, place the short ribs on individual plates and pour the sauce over them. Garnish with the chopped parsley.

Eggplant Spaghetti Rolls

My dad told me about this incredible dish he'd had at an Italian restaurant in San Diego. He described it to me in great detail, saying it was the best Italian dish he'd ever had, so I immediately started taking notes. It turns out it's two of the best Italian classics in one: eggplant parmesan meets spaghetti with tomato sauce. **Serves 6**

2 medium eggplants, peeled and thinly sliced lengthwise

Extra-virgin olive oil

Pink Himalayan salt

7 cups Dad's Famous Pasta Sauce (page 255) or your favorite pasta sauce

1 pound brown rice spaghetti, cooked, drained, and rinsed

¼ cup chopped fresh basil, plus 1 cup whole basil leaves

1½ cups shredded Manchego cheese

4 cups buffalo ricotta

Freshly ground black pepper

3 cups sliced buffalo mozzarella

1 Preheat the oven to 375°F.

2 On 2 or 3 large baking sheets, as needed, arrange the eggplant slices in a single layer. Lightly coat each slice with olive oil and sprinkle with a pinch of salt (if you don't have enough baking sheets, do this step in batches). Bake for 10 to 15 minutes, until the eggplant slices are soft and pliable. Set aside until completely cooled.

3 Pour 1 cup of the pasta sauce on the bottom of a 9 × 13-inch casserole dish.

4 In a large mixing bowl, combine the cooked brown rice spaghetti, 3 cups of the pasta sauce, the chopped basil, 1 cup of the Manchego cheese, all the ricotta, and a pinch each of salt and pepper; mix to combine. Place about ¼ cup of this mixture on one end of an eggplant slice, and roll the eggplant up around it. Repeat with the remaining eggplant slices and ricotta mixture, placing the eggplant rolls evenly in the casserole dish, seam down, until the dish is evenly covered.

5 Top the eggplant rolls with the remaining 3 cups pasta sauce, the slices of buffalo mozzarella, the remaining ½ cup Manchego, and the whole basil leaves. Bake until the cheese is fully melted and sauce is beginning to bubble, 30 to 45 minutes. Let it cool for 10 minutes before serving.

Oat Crust Chicken Pot Pie

Pot pies were a staple in my house when I was growing up; they will always take me back to being a kid, making pot pie one of my favorite meals to this day. I've removed the dairy and the gluten here, so this is right in line with how my family eats on a daily basis. I typically save this dish for the weekends when I have more time to get dinner ready, or I make my crust the day before to save time. **Serves 6**

Crust

3 cups oat flour

6 teaspoons arrowroot powder

¼ teaspoon baking soda

½ teaspoon pink Himalayan salt

½ cup virgin coconut oil, melted, plus more for the pie dish

2 eggs

2 teaspoons cashew butter

Filling

⅓ cup virgin coconut oil

4 medium carrots, diced

1 small yellow onion, chopped

2 cloves garlic, minced

4 stalks celery, diced

½ cup oat flour

4½ cups chicken stock

⅓ cup coconut cream

3 cups diced cooked chicken breast

1 cup frozen peas

2 teaspoons chopped fresh thyme

½ cup chopped fresh parsley

¼ cup chopped fresh sage

1 teaspoon pink Himalayan salt

1 teaspoon freshly ground black pepper

1 **Prepare the crust:** Grease a 9-inch pie dish with coconut oil.

2 In a food processor, combine 2½ cups of the oat flour with the arrowroot powder, baking soda, and salt, and pulse until combined. Add the coconut oil, eggs, and cashew butter and pulse again to combine, making sure to scrape down the sides of the processor. Transfer the mixture to a large bowl.

3 Add the remaining ½ cup flour and fold the mixture together until it is combined and resembles a dough. Split the dough in half and press one half into the greased pie dish (wrap the other half in plastic wrap and set aside in the fridge). Set aside.

(recipe continues)

4 **Make the filling:** Melt the coconut oil in a large sauté pan over medium-high heat. Add the carrots, onion, garlic, and celery and sauté for 10 minutes. Sprinkle the oat flour over the vegetables and cook for an additional 5 minutes, stirring to combine. Gradually whisk in the chicken stock and coconut cream. Let the mixture simmer for 20 minutes, until thickened. Stir in the diced cooked chicken, peas, thyme, parsley, sage, salt, and pepper. Cook for 3 minutes for the flavors to combine. Remove the filling from the heat and pour it into the pie dish.

5 Bake the pot pie: Preheat the oven to 375°F.

6 Remove the other dough ball from the fridge. Place the dough between two sheets of parchment paper, and carefully roll it out to form a 10-inch round (the parchment prevents sticking). Place the round of dough over the top of the pot pie or cut it into strips to create a lattice top. Crimp the edges together with your fingers. Using a knife, cut 4 slits in the top of the crust (not needed for the lattice).

7 Place the pie dish on a baking sheet and bake for 1 hour and 45 minutes, until the filling is bubbly and the crust is golden brown. Let cool slightly before slicing.

Bison and Manchego–Stuffed Artichokes

The idea of stuffing artichokes can be daunting, but it's not that difficult. Cleaning the artichokes is the most time-consuming part, and once that's complete, the rest of the preparation is easy. While stuffed artichokes can take some time to prepare, they also should be enjoyed leisurely and shared with others. It's a very versatile dish and can easily be adapted with different proteins, cheeses, bread crumbs, and herbs.

You can serve simple aioli (page 258) as a dipping sauce. We serve this as one artichoke per person, but they can be left out for an appetizer to be picked on by multiple people. —*Mike* Serves 4

4 globe artichokes

Pink Himalayan salt

Juice of 2 lemons

1 pound ground bison

3 cups gluten-free Italian-seasoned bread crumbs

1 teaspoon grated lemon zest

½ cup grated Manchego cheese

⅓ cup chopped fresh parsley

2 cloves garlic, minced

1 teaspoon chopped fresh oregano

1 tablespoon chopped fresh basil

½ teaspoon freshly ground black pepper

6 tablespoons extra–virgin olive oil

1 Preheat the oven to 350°F.

2 To clean the artichokes, slice off the stems so the globes can sit upright. Then slice off the top 1 inch of each artichoke crosswise.

3 Bring a large pot of salted water to a boil. Add the lemon juice and the artichokes, reduce the heat to a simmer, and cook for 35 minutes. Remove the artichokes from the pot and let them cool upside down for 10 minutes.

4 Meanwhile, in a large sauté pan, sauté the bison, stirring often, until it is browned, about 10 minutes. Set aside.

5 In a medium mixing bowl, combine the bread crumbs, cooked bison, lemon zest, Manchego, parsley, garlic, oregano, basil, 1 teaspoon salt, pepper, and 5 tablespoons of the olive oil. Bring the ingredients together with a spoon until a coarse crumble-like mixture is formed; set aside.

6 With your hands, gently open up and peel back the artichoke leaves, making sure to keep all the leaves intact. Stuff a generous amount of the bison mixture into each opening. Sit the artichokes upright on a baking dish and bake for 20 to 25 minutes, until golden brown.

7 To serve, drizzle the artichokes with the remaining 1 tablespoon olive oil. Enjoy eating them by pulling out stuffed leaves and eating the stuffing and tender bottom part of the artichoke leaves.

Dover Sole
with Lemon Zest

Dover sole is one of my favorite fish for its fall-apart-in-your-mouth feeling. It's so delicate and delicious that it doesn't require many other ingredients. I like the traditional way it's prepared here, lightly breaded (in this case with gluten-free oat flour) and cooked in butter and lemon. 'Nuff said. **Serves 4**

4 large Dover sole fillets

¾ cup oat flour

Pink Himalayan salt

¾ teaspoon freshly ground black pepper

6 tablespoons goat's-milk butter (or your favorite butter)

½ teaspoon grated lemon zest

Juice of ½ lemon

1 Pat the sole fillets dry with paper towels and set them aside.

2 In a medium shallow bowl, stir the flour, 1½ teaspoons salt, and pepper together. Sprinkle each fillet with a big pinch of salt and then coat them in the flour mixture.

3 In a large sauté pan, warm the butter over medium-high heat, stirring it occasionally, until it starts to brown. Place the fillets in the lightly browned butter and cook for 2 minutes on one side, then carefully flip them over and cook for 2 to 3 minutes on the second side. Work in batches if needed. During the last minute of cooking, add the lemon zest and juice to the pan.

4 Remove the fillets from the pan and drizzle the lemon butter sauce over top. Serve immediately.

Shredded Chicken Enchilada Casserole

This is one of my go-tos for serving a big group when I don't have enough time to make an elaborate meal. The prep is painless and the whole dish takes about 45 minutes from start to finish. It's always a hit, and cleanup is minimal with the one-pan setup. **Serves 8**

2 tablespoons avocado oil

1 large yellow onion, sliced

2 poblano chiles or green bell peppers, seeds removed, sliced

2 cloves garlic, minced

1 teaspoon ground cumin

Pink Himalayan salt

Freshly ground black pepper

1 (15-ounce) can pinto beans, drained and rinsed

1 teaspoon smoked paprika

1 teaspoon chili powder

¼ teaspoon onion powder

4 cups shredded cooked chicken thigh meat

1 (14.5-ounce) can black beans, drained and rinsed

1 (14.5-ounce) can diced fire-roasted tomatoes, drained

1 (4-ounce) can diced green chiles

3½ cups jarred enchilada sauce

18 tortillas (I like the Siete brand almond flour)

3 cups grated goat's-milk cheddar cheese

2 medium avocados, diced

¼ cup chopped fresh cilantro

½ cup jarred pico de gallo

1 cup Cashew Crema (page 259)

1   Preheat the oven to 350°F.

2   In a large skillet, warm the avocado oil over medium heat. Add the onion and chiles and sauté for 5 minutes. Add the garlic and continue cooking for 2 more minutes, until fragrant. Add the cumin and a couple pinches each of salt and pepper, and stir to combine. Remove the skillet from the heat and set aside.

3   In a high-powered blender, combine the pinto beans with the smoked paprika, chili powder, onion powder, and a couple pinches each of salt and pepper. Blend until the mixture is smooth and resembles refried beans (add a little water if needed).

4 In a medium mixing bowl, mix together the shredded chicken, black beans, tomatoes, and green chiles until well combined. Add 1 tablespoon of the enchilada sauce to bring everything together, and stir to combine.

5 In a 9 × 13-inch baking dish, spread ½ cup of the enchilada sauce on the bottom and then add a layer of 6 tortillas, making sure to cover the sauce. Next, spread a thin layer of the pinto bean puree over the tortillas. Sprinkle ⅔ cup of the cheese and 1 cup enchilada sauce over the bean puree. Add a layer of the chicken mixture and then a layer of the sautéed peppers and onions.

6 Repeat the layers (except the first layer of sauce) twice more, until all the ingredients are used. Finish by topping with the remaining cheese. Bake for 30 minutes or until the edges are bubbly and the cheese is golden brown.

7 Garnish the casserole with the diced avocado, chopped cilantro, pico de gallo, and dollops of Cashew Crema. Serve immediately.

Slow-Cooker Lasagna

When I discovered I could make lasagna in a slow cooker, my whole world changed! Lasagna is easily one of our family go-tos, and now it's even easier than you could imagine. You really can't mess this up—just throw whatever you want in here. I like zucchini and squash for some veggies, but by all means, leave them out if you want a more traditional lasagna. I know that with this recipe, I'll have my kids' tummies full. **Serves 6**

1 pound ground bison or beef

1 teaspoon pink Himalayan salt

1½ jars (about 40 ounces) tomato sauce

1 medium zucchini, chopped

1 medium yellow squash, chopped

1 package brown rice lasagna noodles

Fresh basil leaves, for garnish

1   Turn your slow cooker on low to cook for 8 hours or on high to cook for 4 hours.

2   In a large skillet, combine the the bison with the salt and sauté over medium-high heat until browned, about 4 minutes. Set aside.

3   Layer your lasagna ingredients in the slow cooker: one third of the tomato sauce, half of the cooked bison, half each of the zucchini and yellow squash, and then half of the noodles covering the top (break them if they're too big).

Repeat with the remaining tomato sauce, bison, zucchini, yellow squash, and noodles to make one more layer. Spread any leftover tomato sauce over top.

4   Cover the cooker and cook, stirring occasionally, on low for 8 hours or on high for 4 hours.

5   Serve hot, garnished with fresh basil leaves. Any leftovers will keep well in the fridge for up to 3 days.

Slow-Roasted Chicken

This chicken is one of the first things I learned to make when I started cooking. Any time guests came over, I would default to a slow-roasted chicken since I could guarantee the tenderness and knew it would never fail me. As simple as it is, people always *ooh* and *ahh* because not only is the presentation impressive, the chicken is incredibly flavorful and the juices are locked in. Be aware: this chicken roasts for 9½ hours, so you'll want to start it in the morning. Your house will smell amazing all day while it roasts. **Serves 4**

8 cloves garlic: 4 minced, 4 whole

1 teaspoon chopped fresh thyme, plus 1 sprig

1 teaspoon chopped fresh rosemary, plus 1 sprig

1 teaspoon chopped fresh basil, plus 2 big leaves

1 tablespoon virgin coconut oil, room temperature

2 teaspoons pink Himalayan salt

½ teaspoon freshly ground black pepper

1 teaspoon grated lemon zest

1 whole chicken (about 4 pounds)

1 large yellow onion, quartered

½ lemon

2 tablespoons balsamic vinegar

1 Preheat the oven to 200°F.

2 In a small bowl, create a paste by mashing together the minced garlic, chopped thyme, rosemary, and basil, then add the coconut oil, salt, pepper, and lemon zest.

3 Place the chicken, breast-side up, in a large Dutch oven or heavy pot. Rub the paste all over the chicken, making sure to get it under the skin as well. In the cavity, place a quarter of the onion, the lemon half, 2 whole cloves garlic, 1 sprig each of thyme and rosemary, and the 2 basil leaves. Scatter the remaining onion quarters and garlic cloves around the chicken in the Dutch oven. Drizzle the balsamic vinegar over the chicken.

4 Cover the pot, place it in the oven, and roast for 9½ hours.

5 Uncover the Dutch oven, raise the oven heat to 425°F, and roast the chicken until the skin crisps, 10 minutes.

Saffron Seafood Cioppino

When the snow is falling outside, there is nothing better than a big, warm bowl of cioppino. Loaded with clams, mussels, and shrimp, full of flavor with pungent saffron, this dish is for seafood lovers. Make the mini Manchego and chive cauliflower biscuits on page 155 to soak up every last drop. **Serves 6**

2 tablespoons extra-virgin olive oil

1 fennel bulb, sliced

1 large sweet onion, chopped

2 large shallots, chopped

2 teaspoons pink Himalayan salt

4 cloves garlic, minced

½ teaspoon saffron threads

¼ teaspoon red pepper flakes

¼ cup tomato paste

1 (28-ounce) can diced tomatoes, with their juice

5 cups chicken stock

½ cup coconut cream

1 bay leaf

1 pound littleneck clams

1 pound mussels

1 pound large shrimp, peeled and deveined

Freshly ground black pepper

¼ cup chopped fresh parsley, for garnish

Lemon wedges, for garnish

1 In a large Dutch oven pot, heat the olive oil over medium heat. Add the fennel, onion, shallots, salt, garlic, saffron, and red pepper flakes; sauté for 10 minutes. Stir in the tomato paste and cook for another 2 minutes. Add the diced tomatoes, with their juice, along with the chicken stock, coconut cream, and bay leaf. Cover the pot and bring to a simmer. Reduce the heat to medium and cook, stirring occasionally, for 25 to 30 minutes for the flavors to come together.

2 Remove 4 cups of the vegetable mixture and pour it into a high-powered blender. Blend on low speed, then turn it up to high and blend until smooth. Return the puree to the pot and cook over medium heat for 5 minutes.

3 Add the clams and mussels to the pot, cover, and cook until they begin to open, 10 minutes. Add the shrimp and simmer until they are cooked and the clams are completely open, 5 minutes.

4 Carefully stir everything together and discard any shellfish that didn't open. Season the stew with salt and black pepper to taste. Spoon the cioppino into serving bowls and garnish each one with chopped parsley and lemon wedges. Serve right away.

Classic Pasta Bolognese

This is always in heavy rotation at my house. During the winter months, it's one of my go-tos when entertaining as well. Always a crowd favorite, pasta bolognese is a hard-to-beat classic dish. I "health-ify" it by using gluten-free brown rice noodles or lentil noodles, but feel free to use your favorite type of pasta. **Serves 6**

2 tablespoons extra-virgin olive oil

2 medium yellow onions, finely chopped

2 large stalks celery, finely chopped

2 large carrots, finely chopped

6 ounces ground beef

6 ounces ground veal

4 ounces pancetta, chopped

½ cup red wine (I like Cabernet)

3 cups chicken stock

3 tablespoons tomato paste

1 cup full-fat coconut milk

Pink Himalayan salt

Freshly ground black pepper

¾ (16-ounce) package gluten-free pasta (I like brown rice spirals)

1 In a large Dutch oven or heavy pot, heat the olive oil over medium heat. Add the onions, celery, and carrots and cook until they are soft, 8 minutes. Then add the beef, veal, and pancetta and cook until the meats are browned, 6 minutes. Add the wine, bring it to a boil, and cook for 1 minute, scraping up any brown bits from the bottom of the pot. Add 2½ cups of the stock and the tomato paste; stir until combined. Simmer for 1 hour and 15 minutes, stirring occasionally.

2 In a small saucepan, warm the coconut milk over medium heat. Slowly add the warm milk to the bolognese, stirring until it is completely combined. Simmer the bolognese, stirring it occasionally, until the milk has been absorbed, 45 minutes. Season it with salt and pepper.

3 Cook the pasta according to the package directions. Drain and then rinse the pasta. Add it to the sauce and stir to combine. If the pasta seems dry, then add the remaining ½ cup stock. Season with salt and pepper to taste. Serve right away. (Any leftovers keep well in the fridge for up to 4 days, if they'll last that long!)

Spicy Peruvian Chicken

The first time I had this dish, the strangest thing happened to me. I had been one of those people who hate cilantro, but it turned me into a cilantro-obsessed person in seconds. I grew up thinking cilantro tasted like soap, but this sauce gave me a newfound appreciation for the love-it-or-hate-it herb. The dish is rich and creamy, yet undeniably fresh and with a good kick of heat. Serve this chicken with the smashed plantains (page 167) and some roasted veggies for a paleo-friendly meal. The chicken is best when marinated for at least 8 hours so definitely try to do that step the night before, or in the morning before heading to work (like me). **Serves 6**

Chicken

3 tablespoons extra-virgin olive oil

¼ cup fresh lime juice (about 2 big limes)

4 large cloves garlic, coarsely chopped

1 tablespoon pink Himalayan salt

2 teaspoons paprika

1 teaspoon freshly ground black pepper

1 tablespoon ground cumin

1 teaspoon dried oregano

2 teaspoons coconut sugar

1 whole chicken (about 4 pounds)

Sauce

¾ cup packed fresh cilantro leaves

¾ cup vegan mayo

2 tablespoons apple cider vinegar

½ teaspoon pink Himalayan salt

3 jalapeños, seeds removed if desired, coarsely chopped

2 large cloves garlic, coarsely chopped

1 tablespoon fresh lime juice (about 1 lime)

⅛ teaspoon freshly ground black pepper

2 tablespoons extra-virgin olive oil

1 **Marinate the chicken:** In a blender, combine the olive oil, lime juice, garlic, salt, paprika, pepper, cumin, oregano, and coconut sugar. Blend on high speed until smooth.

2 Place the chicken in a large baking dish and coat it with the marinade, making sure to get some under the skin and inside the cavity. Let the chicken marinate in the fridge covered for at least 8 hours or overnight.

3 **Roast the chicken:** Preheat the oven to 425°F.

4 While the oven warms up, remove the chicken from the fridge to warm it up slightly. Keep the chicken in the same pan with the marinade still on it and roast the chicken until the skin crisps, 20 minutes. Then reduce the heat to 375°F and cook for 1 hour, until the chicken is completely cooked through and registers 165°F on an instant-read thermometer.

5 **Make the sauce:** While the chicken is roasting, in a blender, combine the cilantro, mayo, apple cider vinegar, salt, jalapeños, garlic, lime juice, and pepper and blend on high speed until well combined. While the blender is still running, slowly drizzle in the olive oil.

6 To serve, carve the chicken and place the meat on a large platter. Pour ½ cup of the sauce over the roasted chicken and use the extra as a dipping sauce.

7 This sauce will keep well in the fridge for up to 5 days, and any leftover chicken is great to throw on a salad or on a sandwich for the following 2 days as well.

Chicken Milanese

I've never met anyone who doesn't love chicken parmesan—it's a classic dish that seems to bring back a fond memory for just about everyone. I remember ordering it when we would go out to eat as a kid and it being smothered in gooey cheese. I always managed to eat every last bite. I couldn't put together a comfort-food cookbook without including some version of "fried" chicken. I love chicken parm, but sometimes I just want the chicken by itself (Milanese) or smothered in pesto or in my Dad's famous pasta sauce, without all the heavy cheese. So here you go—chicken Milanese with a twist. For the classic Milanese, leave the pesto and tomato sauce off. **Serves 4**

1 tablespoon extra-virgin olive oil

4 skinless, boneless chicken breasts

Pink Himalayan salt

Freshly ground black pepper

1½ cups gluten-free bread crumbs

4 cloves garlic, minced

1 tablespoon dried basil

1 teaspoon paprika

3 eggs

2 cups Classic Basil Pesto (page 256) or Dad's Famous Pasta Sauce (page 255), at room temperature

1 Preheat the oven to 425°F. Grease a large baking sheet with the olive oil.

2 Place the chicken breasts on a cutting board and pound them until they are about ¼ inch thick. Season the chicken with salt and pepper.

3 In a medium shallow dish, combine the bread crumbs, garlic, basil, 1½ teaspoons salt, and the paprika. In another medium shallow dish, whisk the eggs together until combined. Dip the chicken breasts first in the eggs, coating them completely, and then cover them in the bread-crumb mixture, wiping off any excess. Place the chicken on the prepared baking sheet.

4 Bake the chicken for 15 minutes, until golden brown. Serve it right away, with Classic Basil Pesto smothered over the top or with Dad's Famous Pasta Sauce and a roasted veggie.

Dad's Meatballs and Famous Pasta Sauce

On Christmas Eve, my dad always made homemade meatballs and sauce. I've kept up the tradition and it's something my whole family looks forward to each year. This recipe is almost identical to my dad's, with the exception of a dairy substitute (I swapped coconut milk for the whole cow's milk). I left white bread in because sometimes ya just gotta do it, especially during the holidays. Of course, feel free to use a gluten-free bread substitute.

Dad and I would both agree that his meatballs are the best because of his secret ingredient: tamari. He was going for the ultimate umami flavor, and he succeeded.

These meatballs cook in the sauce all day, so here is what I like to do: The morning of Christmas Eve, after I've fed my kids breakfast, I make a yummy cup of coffee and, still in my pj's, I get these going. I enlist my kids to mix the meatballs with their hands because they find it fun and gross at the same time, which has them laughing all morning. Serves 6

Dad's Famous Pasta Sauce (page 255)
1 (1-inch-thick) slice white bread, crust removed and cut into cubes

4 large eggs
1 pound ground beef
1 pound ground veal
1 tablespoon chopped fresh basil

2 cloves garlic, minced
2 tablespoons tamari
½ teaspoon pink Himalayan salt
Freshly ground black pepper

1 In a large saucepan, heat up Dad's Famous Pasta Sauce.

2 **Make the meatballs:** Place the bread cubes in a medium bowl. In a small bowl, beat 2 of the eggs. Add the beaten eggs to the bread cubes, and using your hands, mash the eggs and bread together until they are fully combined and form a thick paste-like consistency; set it aside.

(recipe continues)

3 In a small bowl, beat the remaining 2 eggs together.

4 In a large bowl, mix the beef, veal, basil, beaten eggs, garlic, tamari, salt, and a pinch of pepper. Add the egg-soaked bread and mix everything together with your hands until well combined. Roll the mixture into meatballs to the size of your liking (I've been known to make massive meatballs, as big as a fist, or others as small as golf balls). Place them on a large baking sheet.

5 Once the sauce is hot, gently add the meatballs to it, one at a time. Make sure all the meatballs are covered by the sauce. Reduce the heat under the pot to low; it's good to have a few bubbles at the top of your sauce, but any more and you could be burning the sauce. If you see more than 2 or 3 bubbles, reduce the heat. Cover the pot with the lid ajar. Cook all day—up to 8 hours for the flavors to really combine.

6 We like to eat the meatballs as is with the Fried Brussels Sprouts with Pine Nut Crumble and Lemon Vinaigrette (page 170) and Mini Manchego and Chive Cauliflower Biscuits (page 155), but they would also be divine over brown rice spaghetti.

Sides

Roasted Broccolini

My hands-down favorite way to cook veggies is to roast them in the oven. I like my broccolini slightly charred because it brings out a mild nutty flavor. My kids devour broccolini (I can't say the same for other vegetables), so when I make this, I do half without the red pepper flakes for them. **Serves 6**

2 bunches broccolini, leaves removed and ends trimmed

1½ tablespoons extra-virgin olive oil

½ teaspoon pink Himalayan salt

½ teaspoon red pepper flakes

1 tablespoon grated lemon zest

½ teaspoon freshly ground black pepper

1 large shallot, thinly sliced

1   Preheat the oven to 425°F. Line a large baking sheet with foil.

2   Place the broccolini on the baking sheet. Sprinkle it with the olive oil, salt, red pepper flakes, lemon zest, and black pepper, and toss it with your hands to get the oil and spices all over the broccolini. Sprinkle the shallots on top of the broccolini. Roast for 30 minutes, until the broccolini is ever so slightly charred. Serve immediately.

Cajun Fried Okra

I know it's the beginning of fall when I see okra back in the grocery store. If you don't know what okra is, it sort of looks like a thicker green bean and has a mild flavor. I like cooking okra many ways, from sautéing to frying. Here I coat okra pods in oat flour so they'll be gluten-free, then fry them in avocado oil. These little guys are addicting, so you will either love me or hate me for this recipe! **Serves 4**

½ cup full-fat coconut milk

2 pounds okra pods, tops and ends cut off, cut into ½-inch pieces

4 cups avocado oil

½ cup gluten-free bread crumbs

1 cup oat flour

2 teaspoons your favorite Cajun seasoning

¼ teaspoon garlic powder

¼ teaspoon smoked paprika

Pink Himalayan salt

Freshly ground black pepper

2 eggs

Simple Aioli (page 258), for serving

1 In a medium shallow dish, combine the coconut milk with the okra; let it soak for 5 minutes.

2 While the okra is soaking, pour the avocado oil into a large skillet or Dutch oven, making sure it doesn't reach more than halfway up the sides of the pan. You might need more or less depending on the size of your pan. Heat the avocado oil to 350°F, using a deep-fry thermometer to be accurate.

3 Meanwhile, in a medium mixing bowl, combine the bread crumbs, oat flour, Cajun seasoning, garlic powder, smoked paprika, ½ teaspoon salt, and a pinch of pepper; mix well. In another shallow medium dish, whisk the eggs together.

4 Drain the okra, discarding the excess coconut milk. Set up an assembly line: dredge the okra in the eggs, then in the flour mixture, coating each piece well.

5 Working in small batches, carefully add the okra to the hot oil and cook until golden brown, 2 to 3 minutes. As they are cooked, use a slotted spoon to transfer the okra pods to paper towels to drain. Season the okra with salt and pepper and serve with simple aioli alongside.

Spicy Braised Kale

Spending a lot of time in the South made me crave good collard greens all the time. Since I typically grow a lot of kale in my garden, I came up with a midwestern/Italian spin on those braised greens. They are a perfect side to any dish and leave a surprising and satisfying spice in your mouth. —*Mike* **Serves 4**

1 tablespoon extra-virgin olive oil

1½ cups thinly sliced white onion

⅓ cup thinly sliced garlic

1 jalapeño, minced

10 cups loosely packed chopped kale

¼ cup tomato paste

¾ teaspoon red pepper flakes

2 teaspoons white wine vinegar

3 cups chicken stock

¼ teaspoon pink Himalayan salt

¼ teaspoon freshly ground black pepper

1 Heat the olive oil in a Dutch oven over medium heat. Add the onion, garlic, and jalapeño. Cook, stirring constantly, for 10 minutes.

2 Add the kale, tomato paste, red pepper flakes, and white wine vinegar; stir until combined. Cook for an additional 5 minutes.

3 Add the chicken stock, salt, and black pepper; stir to combine. Cover the pot and bring the mixture to a boil. Then reduce the heat and let it simmer for 20 minutes, until the kale is tender. Add more salt and black pepper if needed.

Roasted Sweet Potatoes
with Chili Sauce

This is a delectable balance of sweet potatoes and chile—easily one of my favorite side dishes. Serve the potatoes with the slow-roasted chicken (page 135), the creamy garlic halibut (page 115), or with a salad for a light meal. **Serves 4**

4 medium sweet potatoes, scrubbed

1 tablespoon extra-virgin olive oil

½ teaspoon pink Himalayan salt

½ teaspoon freshly ground black pepper

½ teaspoon chili powder

3 tablespoons raw honey

¼ cup gochujang paste

¼ cup Sriracha

½ tablespoon sesame oil

½ teaspoon red pepper flakes

3 scallions, white and green parts thinly sliced, for garnish

½ tablespoon toasted sesame seeds, for garnish

1 Preheat the oven to 375°F.

2 Slice the sweet potatoes into 2- to 3-inch wedges. Coat them with the olive oil, and sprinkle with the salt and pepper. Place the potato wedges on a baking sheet and roast for 12 minutes.

3 Meanwhile, in a large mixing bowl, combine the chili powder, raw honey, gochujang paste, Sriracha, sesame oil, and red pepper flakes. Stir together to form a smooth, paste-like sauce.

4 Add the roasted sweet potatoes to the sauce and toss to coat. Return the sweet potatoes to the baking sheet and roast for an additional 10 minutes, until tender.

5 To serve, generously garnish the sweet potatoes with the sliced scallions and toasted sesame seeds.

Mini Manchego and Chive Cauliflower Biscuits

Cauliflower might be my favorite vegetable for its versatility alone. I use it for almost everything: cauliflower mac-n-cheese (page 163), cauliflower (pizza) crust (page 116), smoothies, and now biscuits. For these biscuits, cauliflower's somewhat bland flavor picks up the chives and Manchego without letting them overpower. These are the perfect companion for just about any meal. This requires a mini muffin tin but if you don't have one you could spoon dollops onto a greased baking sheet and just bake that way. **Makes 24 mini biscuits**

Virgin coconut oil, for the pan

1 head cauliflower, cored and cut into florets

Pink Himalayan salt

Freshly ground black pepper

3 cloves Roasted Garlic (page 117)

2 eggs, beaten, plus 2 egg whites

½ cup grated Manchego cheese

1 tablespoon chopped fresh chives

¼ cup oat flour

1 tablespoon full-fat coconut milk

1 Preheat the oven to 425°F. Grease a mini muffin tin with coconut oil.

2 Place the cauliflower florets on a large baking sheet, and sprinkle with the salt and pepper. Roast until tender, 12 minutes.

3 Transfer the roasted cauliflower to a food processor, add the roasted garlic, and pulse until finely chopped, about 1 minute.

4 In a large bowl, stir the chopped cauliflower mixture with the beaten eggs and the cheese, ½ teaspoon salt, chives, oat flour, and coconut milk until well combined. In a separate large bowl, beat the egg whites until they form stiff peaks. Fold the whites into the cauliflower mixture.

5 Spoon the batter mixture into the mini muffin tin until the cups are full. Bake until light golden brown, 20 to 25 minutes. Let cool slightly before removing from the muffin tin and placing on a cooling rack. Serve warm. These keep well in an airtight container in the fridge up to 4 days.

Braised Red Cabbage

Cabbage is a powerhouse vegetable for its many health benefits. Packed with vitamin C, it helps with many body functions, including the immune system and the absorption of iron. Sweet yet savory, this dish is packed with flavor. Pair the cabbage with red wine–braised short ribs (page 119), apple butter lamb chops (page 107), or slow-roasted chicken (page 135). **Serves 4**

4 slices bacon, chopped

1 medium yellow onion, sliced

1 (3-inch) cinnamon stick

2 bay leaves

1½ teaspoons pink Himalayan salt

1 medium head red cabbage, cored and thinly sliced

1 small Granny Smith apple, cored and cut into bite-sized pieces

4 cups chicken stock

2 tablespoons red wine vinegar

2 tablespoons raw honey

½ teaspoon freshly ground black pepper

1 In a large Dutch oven, cook the bacon over medium heat for 4 minutes. Add the onion, cinnamon stick, bay leaves, and salt. Cook, stirring occasionally, until the onion softens, 5 minutes.

2 Raise the heat to medium-high. Add the cabbage and cook, stirring constantly, until it has wilted, 5 minutes. Then add the apple, chicken stock, vinegar, honey, and pepper; stir to combine. Cover the pot and cook, stirring occasionally, until the cabbage is tender, 5 minutes. Uncover the pot and bring the mixture to a boil. Continue to cook, stirring occasionally, until most of the liquid has been absorbed and what's left is reduced to a sauce-like consistency, 1 hour.

3 Discard the bay leaves and cinnamon stick. Serve immediately.

Coconut Creamed Spinach

Creamed spinach reminds me of my early days in Chicago, when I frequently ate at a particular steak house and always ordered the creamed spinach. I never felt great afterward (thanks to a casein sensitivity), so I figured out how to make the dairy-free version. This dish has become a Christmas Day tradition in my house over the past few years, and I don't see it stopping any time soon. **Serves 4**

3 tablespoons virgin coconut oil

2 shallots, diced

3 cloves garlic, chopped

Pinch of red pepper flakes (optional)

½ cup chicken stock

1½ cups coconut cream

2 teaspoons oat flour

1 (8-ounce) bag fresh baby spinach, coarsely chopped

Pinch of ground nutmeg

1 teaspoon chopped fresh thyme

1 tablespoon chopped fresh basil

Pink Himalayan salt

Freshly ground black pepper

1 In a large sauté pan, warm the coconut oil over medium heat. Add the shallots, garlic, and red pepper flakes (if using); sauté until fragrant, 5 minutes. Add the chicken stock and coconut cream, and bring to a simmer. Gradually whisk in the oat flour. Let the mixture cook until it thickens, 8 minutes.

2 Add the spinach, nutmeg, thyme, and basil to the coconut mixture; mix well. Cook for an additional 10 minutes for the flavors to combine. (You can add more stock if the mixture becomes too thick.)

3 Add salt and pepper to taste. Serve hot.

Squash Fritters

I love these little guys. They are essentially a squash pancake and are great by themselves, with a dollop of yogurt on top, or as a dinner side with any protein and veggie. **Makes 5**

1 medium zucchini, grated

1 medium yellow squash, grated

¾ teaspoon pink Himalayan salt

½ cup oat flour

2 eggs, lightly beaten

3 scallions, white and light green parts, chopped

¼ teaspoon freshly ground black pepper

4 teaspoons virgin coconut oil

1   Place the zucchini and yellow squash in a colander, and sprinkle with ½ teaspoon of the salt. Let sit for 10 minutes to draw out the moisture. Then place the vegetables in a nut milk bag or wrap them in a clean kitchen towel, and squeeze out the extra moisture over the sink. Transfer the drained squash mixture to a large bowl. Add the flour, eggs, scallions, remaining ¼ teaspoon salt, and the pepper. Stir until well combined.

2   In a large skillet, warm 2 teaspoons of the coconut oil over medium heat. Pour ¼ cup of the batter into the skillet and press down on it with the back of a spoon or the bottom of a measuring cup. Cook until the fritter is golden brown on the bottom, about 4 minutes. Then flip it over and cook until the other side is also golden brown, 4 to 6 minutes. Place on a plate covered to keep warm while you repeat with the remaining batter to make 4 fritters.

Simple Roasted Beets

Beets and the colder months go hand in hand. I like them roasted with lemon and thyme to balance out their natural sweetness. **Serves 6**

8 medium beets (any color)

2 tablespoons extra-virgin olive oil

2 lemons, halved

10 sprigs fresh thyme

½ teaspoon pink Himalayan salt

½ teaspoon freshly ground black pepper

1 Preheat the oven to 400°F.

2 Cut the tops off the beets and rinse the beets in a colander (do not peel them). Place the beets in a 9 × 11-inch roasting pan and coat them with the olive oil.

3 Squeeze both lemons directly over the beets, then place the lemon halves in the pan as well. Scatter the thyme sprigs all over the beets. Season the beets with the salt and pepper, and cover the pan tightly with foil.

4 Roast the beets for 35 minutes, until a paring knife slides into them easily. Uncover the pan and let the beets cool for 10 minutes.

5 Once the beets are easy to handle, wrap each one in paper towels and peel off the skin by rubbing it with the paper towel (the skin should come right off). Once all the beets are peeled, slice them or cut them into pieces. Serve them as a side right away, or cool them in the fridge and use in salads. Beets keep well in the fridge up to 3 days.

Roasted Leeks

Leeks look like large scallions and have a flavor that's similar to a shallot. When roasted, the onion flavor subsides and they become sweet. I love these paired with steak and a roasted vegetable. **Serves 4**

2 large leeks, tough green ends trimmed

1 teaspoon extra-virgin olive oil

Pink Himalayan salt

Freshly ground black pepper

1 Preheat the oven to 425°F.

2 Cut the leeks in half lengthwise. Rinse them liberally under cold running water, making sure to get all the dirt and sand out of them while keeping the halves intact. Pat them dry.

3 Place the leeks cut-side up in a medium baking dish. Coat them with the olive oil and season with 2 big pinches of salt and 1 big pinch of pepper. Roast until they are tender and golden brown, 35 minutes. Serve immediately.

Cauliflower Mac-n-Cheese

I consider this recipe to be a home run—not only for my kids, who love it, but also for me. Both my kids and I are obsessed with macaroni and cheese, but the dairy and white flour pasta messes up all of our stomachs. I've added cauliflower to this recipe and I promise, you can't taste it, but you do get all the health benefits. This is gooey and rich, everything you want in a mac-n-cheese, except your body will also thank you. **Serves 4**

½ (16-ounce) package brown rice penne

1 head cauliflower, cored and cut into florets

8 ounces goat's-milk cheddar cheese

3 tablespoons goat's-milk butter

½ teaspoon pink Himalayan salt

¼ teaspoon freshly ground black pepper

1 Cook the penne according to the package directions. Drain and rinse. Return the penne to the same pot.

2 Place the cauliflower in a food processor and pulse until it is finely grated. Add cauliflower to the cooked pasta in the pot. Add the cheese to the food processor and pulse until it is finely grated. Combine the cheese with the pasta and cauliflower.

3 Place the pot over medium-low heat, add the butter, salt, and pepper, and cook until the butter has melted and the flavors have combined, 5 minutes. Serve right away.

Thanksgiving Day Stuffing

My favorite part of Thanksgiving has always been the stuffing. My local store sells cubed gluten-free bread for stuffing, but if you can't find any, just get a loaf of gluten-free bread, dice it, and leave it on the counter for a few days to dry out. **Serves 8**

¾ cup extra-virgin olive oil, plus more for the baking dish and drizzling

¾ pound dry gluten-free bread cubes

7 celery stalks, finely chopped (about 1 cup)

2 Fuji or Gala apples, cored and finely chopped

¾ pound sweet Italian chicken sausage meat removed from casing, finely chopped

1 large yellow onion, finely chopped (about 1½ cups)

2 large cloves garlic, minced

1 teaspoon finely chopped fresh sage

1 tablespoon finely chopped fresh rosemary

1 tablespoon finely chopped fresh thyme

1 teaspoon pink Himalayan salt

1 teaspoon fresh ground black pepper

2¾ cups chicken stock

3 eggs, beaten

1   Preheat the oven to 375°F. Grease a 9 × 11-inch baking dish with olive oil.

2   In a large bowl, toss together the bread cubes, celery, apples, sausage, and onion until combined.

3   In another large bowl, combine the garlic, sage, rosemary, thyme, salt, pepper, chicken stock, eggs, and the ¾ cup of olive oil. Whisk together until well combined. Pour this mixture over the bread cube mixture and toss to combine. Pour into the prepared baking dish, and drizzle some olive oil over the top.

4   Cover the baking dish with foil and bake for 1 hour. Remove the foil and bake for another 35 minutes, until golden brown. Serve hot.

Butternut Squash Mash
with Roasted Garlic

The past few Thanksgivings, I've made this in place of mashed potatoes and not one person has been upset about the switch. Butternut squash is slightly sweeter than the traditional mashed potatoes, so load up these guys with butter and garlic for the perfect sweet and savory side. **Serves 6**

6 tablespoons goat's-milk butter, at room temperature, divided

2 large butternut squash, halved, seeds removed

2 cloves Roasted Garlic (see 117), minced

Pink Himalayan salt

1 Preheat the oven to 415°F. Line a large baking sheet with foil.

2 Spread 4 tablespoons of the butter over the cut sides of 4 butternut squash halves; place the squash face-down on the prepared baking sheet. Roast until the squash are fork-tender, 40 to 45 minutes. Let them cool for 10 minutes.

3 Scoop the squash flesh out of the shells (discard the shells) and put it into a large pot. Add the remaining 2 tablespoons butter, the roasted garlic, and 2 big pinches of salt. Cook over medium heat for 5 minutes for the flavors to combine.

Smashed Plantains

Simple and sweet, these plantains don't need much. They are flavorful on their own, and frying them only brings out their delicious flavor even more. Sprinkle the plantains with salt and you have yourself an easy snack or a nice side to serve with the spicy peruvian chicken (page 140). **Serves 4**

½ cup virgin coconut oil

2 plantains, peeled and cut into 1-inch pieces

Pink Himalayan salt

1 In a large sauté pan, heat the coconut oil over medium-high heat. Add the plantains and cook for 3 to 4 minutes on each side, until golden brown.

2 Remove the plantains from the oil and place them on a paper towel. Flatten each piece by pressing down on it with the back of a spoon. Dip each plantain piece in a bowl of water. Return them to the sauté pan and fry them for 1 minute on each side.

3 Remove the plantains from the sauté pan, sprinkle with salt, and serve.

Roasted Maple Balsamic Acorn Squash

This dish was inspired by one I was served at a restaurant outside of Chicago when I was pregnant with Saylor; it was an explosion of flavor in my mouth and I will never forget it. Acorn squash, naturally sweet, and balsamic vinegar created the perfect flavor pairing I never knew I needed. **Serves 4**

1 large acorn squash, halved, seeds removed

2 tablespoons extra–virgin olive oil

2 tablespoons pure maple syrup

½ teaspoon pink Himalayan salt

2 tablespoons Balsamic vinegar

1 Preheat the oven to 400°F. Line a large baking sheet with foil.

2 Cut the squash halves into 1-inch-thick slices lengthwise, discarding the ends. Spread the slices evenly on the prepared baking sheet.

3 In a small bowl, whisk the olive oil, maple syrup, and salt together. Coat the squash with the mixture. Drizzle the balsamic vinegar over top. Roast the squash for 25 minutes, until fork-tender.

Fried Brussels Sprouts
with Pine Nut Crumble and Lemon Vinaigrette

This dish has been a go-to of mine during the fall and winter months for years. I've even made it on Thanksgiving. Fried in avocado oil, these sprouts aren't heavy. The lemon vinaigrette is the perfect tangy touch with the nice bite from the crispy sprouts. **Serves 4**

Brussels Sprouts

Avocado oil, for frying

1 pound Brussels sprouts, trimmed and cut in half, at room temperature

Pink Himalayan salt

Lemon Vinaigrette

1 tablespoon chopped fresh basil

1 teaspoon chopped fresh thyme

1 teaspoon champagne vinegar

1 clove garlic, minced

¼ cup raw honey

2 tablespoons fresh lemon juice, plus zest of 1 lemon

½ teaspoon Dijon mustard

1 teaspoon vegan mayo (or your favorite mayo)

2 tablespoons extra–virgin olive oil

Pink Himalayan salt

Freshly ground black pepper

Pine Nut Crumble

1 cup finely chopped roasted cauliflower (see page 155)

¼ cup pine nuts, toasted

¼ cup finely chopped fresh parsley

Pink Himalayan salt

Freshly ground black pepper

1 **Fry the Brussels sprouts:** Line a large bowl with paper towels, and set it aside.

2 Fill a medium-sized Dutch oven a little less than halfway with avocado oil, and heat it over medium heat. Bring the oil to 375°F (check it with a digital thermometer).

3 Add half of the Brussels sprouts and raise the heat a little to compensate for the oil temperature dropping slightly. Fry the Brussels sprouts, stirring constantly, until they are golden brown and smell nutty, 10 to 12 minutes, until golden brown. Use a slotted spoon to transfer the fried sprouts to the paper-towel-lined bowl. Sprinkle them with salt. Add the remaining sprouts to the oil and repeat the process.

4 **Make the vinaigrette:** In a small mixing bowl, combine the basil and thyme. Whisk in the champagne vinegar, garlic, honey, lemon juice and zest, mustard, mayo, and olive oil until fully combined. Season with salt and pepper to taste.

5 **Make the garnish:** In a small bowl, mix together the cauliflower, pine nuts, parsley, and a pinch each of salt and pepper. Set aside.

6 To assemble the dish, place the fried sprouts in a serving dish and drizzle the vinaigrette all over the top. Garnish with the pine nut crumble.

Parsnip Fries
with Simple Aioli

I'm a big fan of any French fry alternative, but roasted parsnips dipped in fresh homemade aioli is the recipe I keep coming back to. Their mild flavor takes on the smoked paprika and turmeric here perfectly. **Serves 6**

4 large parsnips, peeled and cut into ¼-inch-thick sticks

¼ cup extra-virgin olive oil

1 teaspoon ground turmeric

1 teaspoon dried thyme

1 teaspoon smoked paprika

1 teaspoon pink Himalayan salt

½ cup Simple Aioli (page 258), for dipping

1 Preheat the oven to 415°F.

2 On a large baking sheet, toss the parsnips with the olive oil. Sprinkle with the turmeric, thyme, paprika, and salt, and toss again to coat them well. Roast the parsnips for 20 minutes, until golden brown. Serve immediately, with the simple aioli alongside.

Quick
Bites

Cauliflower Buffalo Bites

If I were a snack, this is what I would be: a vegetable smothered in something spicy, then drenched in homemade ranch. Sure, you can find a recipe for these guys just about anywhere, but I've included them because they're my favorite snack. **Serves 4**

3 tablespoons plus 1 teaspoon virgin coconut oil, melted

½ cup oat flour

1 tablespoon garlic powder

½ teaspoon pink Himalayan salt

1 head cauliflower, cored and cut into bite-sized pieces

½ cup hot sauce, such as Frank's Red Hot

1 cup Ranch Dressing (page 263; optional)

1 Preheat the oven to 450°F. Grease a baking sheet with 1 teaspoon melted coconut oil.

2 In a large bowl, combine the oat flour, ¼ cup of water, 1 tablespoon of the coconut oil, the garlic powder, and the salt until well combined. Add the cauliflower and toss to coat. Place the cauliflower on the baking sheet and bake for 15 minutes.

3 Meanwhile, in another large bowl, combine the hot sauce with the remaining 2 tablespoons coconut oil.

4 Add the cauliflower to the hot sauce mixture and toss to combine. Return the cauliflower to the baking sheet and bake for an additional 25 minutes, until golden brown. Let cool slightly before serving with ranch as a dipping sauce or just as is.

Sweet Potato Tater Tots

My kids, like most kids, will eat something one day then hate it the next. That can make snacks challenging. For some reason, these tater tots are always a safe bet, so I make them often. My kids have to have ketchup to accompany them, but I'll eat them plain. **Makes about 35 tater tots**

1 tablespoon avocado oil, plus more for the pan

2 medium sweet potatoes, peeled

½ teaspoon onion powder

½ teaspoon paprika

2 eggs, beaten

2 tablespoons oat flour

¼ teaspoon pink Himalayan salt

1 cup gluten-free panko bread crumbs

1 Preheat the oven to 375°F. Grease a large baking sheet with avocado oil.

2 In a large mixing bowl, grate the sweet potatoes on a cheese grater to get them finely grated. Wrap the sweet potatoes in a clean kitchen towel and squeeze out any moisture. Return the sweet potatoes to the mixing bowl.

3 Add the onion powder, paprika, eggs, oat flour, and salt to the grated sweet potatoes. Mix using a spoon until a very sticky mixture is formed. Using your hands, roll out tablespoon-sized tots. Place the bread crumbs in a shallow medium dish and coat each tater tot in the crumbs.

4 Spread out the coated tater tots evenly on the baking sheet and drizzle the avocado oil over each tot (this will help with browning). Bake for 15 minutes, then flip each tater tot over and bake for an additional 10 to 15 minutes, until they are golden brown and crispy.

Bacon-Wrapped Butternut Squash

I've been making this for years. It will always remind me of living in Chicago—I used to make this when my mom would come over to watch football games with me while my babies were crawling around. These are some of my favorite memories. **Serves 6**

1 pound butternut squash

½ pound sliced bacon

2 tablespoons coconut sugar

1 teaspoon ground cinnamon

1 Preheat the oven to 375°F. Line a baking sheet with foil.

2 Cut the ends off the squash and peel it. Cut the squash in half lengthwise and remove the seeds. Cut the squash into 1- to 1½-inch cubes.

3 Cut the bacon strips in half lengthwise. Wrap each piece of squash with a piece of bacon, then place it on the baking sheet seam-side down. (You can secure each piece with a toothpick—this also makes for easy grab and go.) Make sure to leave a little room between the pieces of squash/bacon.

4 In a small bowl, combine the coconut sugar and cinnamon. Sprinkle the mixture over the squash/bacon pieces.

5 Bake until the squash is fork-tender and the bacon is crispy, 30 minutes. Let cool slightly before serving.

6 Set out for a party, these will keep well for a couple of hours. I've also saved them in an airtight container in the fridge and warmed them up the next day.

Seven-Layer Bean Dip
with Spiced Cashew Crema

I can't go through football season without making this dip numerous times. It's perfect for entertaining at home or for bringing to a friend's house. Be sure to make it in a clear dish so everyone can see the multiple layers. **Serves 6**

1½ cups ground beef

1 teaspoon ground cumin

1 teaspoon chili powder

Pink Himalayan salt

1 (14-ounce) can refried black beans

2 cups Simple Guacamole (page 245)

1 cup Spiced Cashew Crema (recipe follows)

1 cup diced cherry tomatoes

¼ cup diced scallions, white and green parts

¼ cup chopped fresh cilantro

⅓ cup chopped jalapeños (optional)

Tortilla chips, for serving (I like the Siete brand salted)

1   In a medium sauté pan, cook the ground beef over medium-high heat until it is browned. Drain off any excess liquid, and season the beef with the cumin, chili powder, and a big pinch of salt. Set the beef aside in the fridge to cool slightly until you're ready to assemble the dip.

2   In a glass loaf pan, layer the refried beans, guacamole, ground beef, and ½ cup of the Spiced Cashew Crema.

3   Top with the tomatoes, scallions, cilantro, remaining Spiced Cashew Crema, and the jalapeños (if using). Chill covered for a couple hours in the fridge or serve right away. Serve with tortilla chips.

SPICED CASHEW CREMA

Makes about 1 cup

1 cup raw cashews
1 tablespoon avocado oil
1 tablespoon fresh lime juice
½ teaspoon pink Himalayan salt
1 teaspoon smoked paprika
½ teaspoon ground cumin

1   Place the cashews, avocado oil, lime juice, salt, paprika, and cumin in a high-powered blender. Add ⅓ cup of water and blend until smooth, 2 minutes. This keeps well in the fridge up to 5 days.

Loaded Sweet Potato Skins

Growing up, I remember my mom loving baked potatoes and making them often. I don't eat potatoes very much, but I do love a good sweet potato here and there (they don't spike blood sugar as much as regular potatoes do). This dish was inspired by my mom—someone who always makes me feel comforted. **Serves 8**

5 medium sweet potatoes, scrubbed clean

1 tablespoon extra-virgin olive oil

Pink Himalayan salt

Freshly ground black pepper

⅓ cup shredded goat's-milk cheddar cheese

½ cup shredded Manchego cheese

⅓ cup Cashew Crema (page 259)

8 slices bacon, cooked and crumbled

1 large avocado, diced

½ cup halved grape tomatoes

⅓ cup canned black beans, drained and rinsed

2 tablespoons chopped fresh chives, for garnish

1 Preheat the oven to 400°F. Line a large baking sheet with foil.

2 Cut the sweet potatoes in half lengthwise, then drizzle them with the olive oil and season them with a big pinch each of salt and pepper. Place the sweet potatoes, cut-side up, on the lined baking sheet and bake for 40 minutes or until tender. Remove the baking sheet from the oven and let the potatoes cool a bit.

3 When the potatoes are cool enough to handle, scoop out the potato flesh, leaving a shell with a thin layer of sweet potato inside. (Save the sweet potato flesh in an airtight container to use for Sweet Potato Crackers, see page 186.)

4 Place the skins back on the baking sheet and sprinkle the cheddar and Manchego cheeses evenly over the inside of each potato skin. Bake until the cheese is melted, 10 minutes. Remove the sweet potato skins from the oven.

5 To assemble the loaded sweet potatoes, top each sweet potato skin with a dollop of Cashew Crema and garnish with the bacon, avocado, tomatoes, black beans, and chives.

Spicy Deviled Eggs

This is a twist on a classic favorite. I've kicked it up a notch here with spice. Every time we get family or friends together, I make half of these deviled eggs according to the recipe and half without the Sriracha. The spice is subtle and you'd be surprised how many more people reach for the spicy version over the traditional guys. **Makes 12 eggs**

12 eggs

6 tablespoons vegan mayo

1 teaspoon yellow mustard

4 teaspoons Sriracha

Pink Himalayan salt

Freshly ground black pepper

1 Bring a large pot of water to a boil; add the eggs and cook for 13 minutes. Remove and run the eggs under cold water to cool them.

2 Cut the eggs in half lengthwise and scoop the yolks into a medium bowl. Set the whites aside. Add the mayo, mustard, Sriracha, a big pinch of salt, and a pinch of pepper to the yolks. Mix well. Spoon the yolk mixture into each cavity in the whites. Serve right away or chill in fridge covered up to 3 days.

Coffee Energy Bites

These are great for a morning or afternoon snack when you just need a little pick-me-up. I like to take them to the office with me to get through a busy day. **Makes 14**

¼ cup finely chopped raw almonds

⅔ cup almond flour

½ cup creamy raw almond butter

1 tablespoon instant coffee granules

¼ cup vanilla protein powder

¼ cup pure maple syrup

¼ teaspoon pure vanilla extract

1 to 2 teaspoons almond milk

½ cup shredded unsweetened coconut

1   In a large bowl, combine the almonds, almond flour, almond butter, coffee granules, protein powder, maple syrup, vanilla, and almond milk. Stir together until well combined (I like to use my hands for this).

2   Roll the dough into golf-ball-sized balls and place them on a baking sheet. Place the shredded coconut in a shallow dish. Roll each ball in the coconut and then return it to the baking sheet. Place the baking sheet in the fridge to chill for at least 1 hour for the bites to firm up before you eat one.

3   These bites keep well in a ziplock bag in the fridge up to 14 days.

Sweet Potato Crackers

I know the thought of making your own crackers seems a bit daunting, but trust me, if I can make these, you can, too. It's hard to beat homemade crackers—they taste so flavorful and fresh. The only thing you have to make sure of is to really spread your dough out so you get thin crackers that are easy to snap into squares once they're baked. **Makes about 6 cups**

Virgin coconut oil, for the baking sheet

1 cup cooked sweet potato flesh (or 1 cup canned sweet potato puree)

1½ cups almond flour

½ cup ground flaxseed

2½ teaspoons baking powder

½ cup arrowroot powder

½ teaspoon pink Himalayan salt

1   Preheat the oven to 350°F. Grease an 18 × 13-inch baking sheet with the coconut oil.

2   Puree the sweet potato in a high-powered blender. Then drain off excess liquid using a cheesecloth to squeeze as much liquid out as possible; discard the liquid and put the drained puree in a large bowl.

3   In the large bowl, mix the sweet potato puree with the almond flour, flaxseed, baking powder, arrowroot, and salt until well combined. Press the dough evenly over the prepared baking sheet, making sure to cover the entire sheet so that the dough is as thin as possible. Use a paring knife to score the dough into 1-inch square crackers (so that they will be easy to break apart after they've been cooked—but don't completely cut through them here).

4   Bake, turning the baking sheet around halfway through, until golden brown and the crackers in the middle of the pan are set, 25 minutes.

5   Remove the baking sheet from the oven and let the crackers cool slightly before breaking it into individual pieces. Store them in an airtight container on the counter up to 7 days.

Cashew Butter Bars

This bar has two layers, one smooth and one crunchy, to make the perfect bite. I prefer homemade bars to store-bought because they contain no additives. This recipe makes for effortless snacking, and the bars will keep well in a ziplock bag in the freezer for up 2 months. **Makes 16 bars**

Base
2¼ cups almond flour
¾ cup cashew butter

Top
1 cup coarsely chopped raw cashews
½ cup sunflower seeds
½ cup hemp seeds
¼ cup chia seeds
¼ cup raw honey
1 cup chopped pitted dried tart cherries

1 **Make the base:** Using your hands, mix the almond flour and cashew butter together in a medium bowl. Evenly press the mixture into a 9 × 9-inch baking dish. Set it aside in the fridge to chill for at least 10 minutes or up to 30 minutes.

2 **Add the top:** In a large bowl, mix the cashews, sunflower seeds, hemp seeds, chia seeds, honey, and cherries together until combined. Gently spread the mixture over the cashew butter base, pressing down to make sure the top sticks to the bottom. Place the baking dish in the freezer for at least 1 hour or up to 3 hours, then cut the bar into individual pieces.

3 Store the bars in a ziplock bag in the fridge for up to 2 weeks or in the freezer for up to 2 months.

CASHEW
BUTTER BARS

ALMOND CHERRY
DATE BARS

Almond Cherry Date Bars

Bars will forever be my travel companion—I never leave home without one in my purse. I love a bar with nuts for protein and dried fruit for a touch of sweetness. To make these last longer, throw them in the freezer and just defrost one an hour or so before you want to enjoy it. **Makes 24 bars**

1 cup pitted Medjool dates

2 cups pitted dried tart cherries

2 cups raw almonds

½ teaspoon ground cinnamon

¼ teaspoon ground cardamom

½ cup toasted grated coconut

1   Line a small baking sheet with parchment paper.

2   Place the dates and dried cherries in a food processor and process until a sticky paste is formed, 2 minutes. Place the paste in a large mixing bowl.

3   Add the almonds to the food processor and process until they are coarsely chopped. Add the almonds, cinnamon, and cardamom to the date mixture. Using your hands, knead the mixture together until combined.

4   Place the paste in the center of the prepared baking sheet and press it evenly into a flat rectangular shape. Sprinkle the toasted coconut over the top and press it firmly to get it to stick.

5   Place the baking sheet in the fridge and chill for 15 minutes. Then remove it and cut the bar into whatever shapes and sizes you like.

6   Store the bars in a ziplock bag in the fridge for up to 2 weeks or in the freezer up to a month.

Desserts

Carrot Cake Cupcakes
with Cashew Frosting

Carrot cake will forever be one of my favorite desserts. These cupcakes with cashew frosting are the next best thing. I would argue that because they're both gluten-free and dairy-free, these aren't actually that bad for you, so go ahead and indulge. **Makes 12 cupcakes**

Cupcakes

1 cup almond flour

½ cup oat flour

½ teaspoon baking soda

½ teaspoon baking powder

½ teaspoon pink Himalayan salt

1½ teaspoons ground cinnamon

½ teaspoon ground ginger

⅛ teaspoon ground nutmeg

2 eggs

¼ cup virgin coconut oil, melted

1 teaspoon fresh lemon juice

½ cup pure maple syrup

¼ cup coconut cream

½ teaspoon pure vanilla extract

2 cups grated carrots

Cashew Frosting

1½ cups raw cashews

1 tablespoon pure maple syrup

1 teaspoon ground cinnamon

Pink Himalayan salt

1 **Make the cupcakes:** Preheat the oven to 350°F. Line the cups of a 12-cup muffin tin with paper or silicone liners.

2 In a large bowl, mix the almond flour, oat flour, baking soda, baking powder, salt, cinnamon, ginger, and nutmeg until well combined.

3 In another large bowl, whisk together the eggs, coconut oil, lemon juice, maple syrup, coconut cream, and vanilla. Fold in the carrots. Add the dry ingredients and mix to combine.

4 Spoon the batter into the prepared muffin tin, filling the cups almost full. Bake until a toothpick inserted in the center of a cupcake comes out clean, 15 minutes.

5 Remove the cupcakes from the tin and let them cool completely on a wire rack, at least 1 hour.

6 **Make the frosting:** When the cupcakes are completely cool, combine the cashews, maple syrup, cinnamon, a pinch of salt, and ¼ cup of water in a high-powered blender. Blend on high speed until completely smooth, 2 minutes.

7 Place the frosting in a ziplock bag and cut off one corner of the bag. Squeeze the frosting onto each cupcake until the top is completely covered.

8 The cupcakes will keep well in an airtight container at room temp for up to 5 days.

Sunflower Butter Fudge

This fudge reminds me of my junior high school days, when I lived in Barrington, Illinois. After school, I would ride the bus to visit my step-grandma, and we would catch up on the day over some fudge and Diet Coke (ugh). Those were the days: not a care in the world. Sunflower butter is made from sunflower seeds, so nut allergies are welcome here! **Makes about 40 squares**

Chocolate Layer

1 cup dark chocolate chips

⅓ cup virgin coconut oil

½ cup almond butter

½ teaspoon pure vanilla extract

2 teaspoons pure maple syrup

Pumpkin Layer

1 cup sunflower butter

½ cup virgin coconut oil, melted

1 tablespoon pumpkin pie spice

1 teaspoon ground cinnamon

2 tablespoons pure maple syrup

1 teaspoon pure vanilla extract

1 Line a 9 × 4-inch loaf pan with parchment paper, having it come up the sides as well.

2 **Make the chocolate layer:** In a medium saucepan, combine the chocolate chips, coconut oil, almond butter, vanilla, and maple syrup. Stir over medium-low heat until smooth. Then remove the pan from the heat and pour the batter into the prepared loaf pan. Freeze for 15 minutes.

3 **Meanwhile, make the pumpkin layer:** In a large bowl, mix the sunflower butter, coconut oil, pumpkin pie spice, cinnamon, maple syrup, and vanilla together until combined. Pour this over the chocolate layer.

4 Freeze the loaf for at least 1 hour. Remove from the loaf pan using the parchment paper and slice into 40 squares. The squares will keep well in an airtight container in the fridge for up to 2 weeks.

Skillet Cookie

Who doesn't love one big-a** cookie?! For some reason, it tastes better when it's this giant. Warm it up (or eat it right out of the oven) and spoon some vanilla coconut ice cream on top. **Serves 8**

½ cup virgin coconut oil, plus more for the skillet, at room temperature

⅔ cup coconut sugar

2 eggs

2 teaspoons pure vanilla extract

2 cups almond flour

½ teaspoon pink Himalayan salt

½ teaspoon baking soda

1 cup dark chocolate chips

½ cup Vanilla Coconut Ice Cream (page 217)

1 Preheat the oven to 350°F. Grease a 12-inch cast-iron skillet with coconut oil.

2 In a large mixing bowl, beat the coconut oil and sugar together until smooth. Add the eggs, one at a time, beating after each one, then add the vanilla. Next, add the flour, salt, and baking soda. Fold in the chocolate chips.

3 Spread the batter evenly in the cast-iron skillet and bake the cookie for 30 minutes, until golden brown.

4 While it's still warm, scoop servings of the cookie from the skillet into bowls and enjoy it right away, with Vanilla Coconut Ice Cream on top.

Olive Oil Cake

Olive oil cake is a traditional Mediterranean dessert. It's light and moist, similar to angel food cake. I love having a slice of this cake for an afternoon pick-me-up when a sweet craving hits. Since it's so fresh and airy, it satisfies my sweet tooth without putting me in a food coma. It's even better with a cup of tea or coffee! The hint of orange will make this a new sweet favorite. If you don't have an orange on hand, you can use lemon or even grapefruit zest. **Serves 8**

5 tablespoons extra-virgin olive oil, plus more for the pan

5 eggs

½ teaspoon pink Himalayan salt

1 cup coconut sugar

2 tablespoons almond milk

1 teaspoon almond extract

1 teaspoon pure vanilla extract

½ tablespoon grated orange zest

2 cups almond flour

¼ teaspoon ground nutmeg

½ cup slivered almonds

1   Preheat the oven to 350°F. Grease a 9 × 9-inch cake pan with olive oil.

2   Separate the egg yolks and whites, placing them in separate large mixing bowls.

3   Add the salt to the egg whites. Using a hand mixer or a stand mixer, beat the whites on medium speed until stiff peaks form, 2 minutes. Set aside.

4   Add the coconut sugar and the almond milk to the yolks. Whisk until the mixture is smooth and fluffy, 5 minutes. Then add the olive oil, almond extract, vanilla, and orange zest; beat until combined.

5   In another large mixing bowl, mix the almond flour and nutmeg together. Stir the yolk mixture into the flour mixture until well combined. Then gently fold the egg whites into the batter, being careful not to deflate the whites. Transfer the batter to the prepared cake pan.

6   Knock the pan on the counter or a wall a couple of times to release any air bubbles. Sprinkle the almonds over the top of the cake. Bake until a toothpick inserted in the center comes out clean, 30 to 35 minutes.

7   Let the cake cool completely before removing it from the pan. Then enjoy it right away or save it for later in an airtight container on the counter up to 5 days.

Individual Chocolate Mousse Pots

This one is for my chocolate lovers. Deep and rich, these are the choice for those times when you want something incredibly decadent. Coconut milk subs for dairy here, leaving an ever-so-slight hint of coconut flavor in your mouth. Enjoy the mousse straight up or with a big scoop of vanilla coconut ice cream. Make sure you get good-quality eggs: the yolks will remain raw, so you want them to be fresh. **Serves 6**

1 cup full-fat coconut milk

2 egg yolks

1½ teaspoons pure vanilla extract

¼ cup pure maple syrup

1 cup unsweetened chocolate chips

Pink Himalayan salt

Vanilla Coconut Ice Cream (optional; page 217)

1 In a small saucepan, simmer the coconut milk until it's hot but not boiling; the milk should be just barely starting to bubble around the edges.

2 Meanwhile, combine the egg yolks, vanilla, maple syrup, chocolate chips, and a pinch of salt in a high-powered blender and blend until smooth.

3 Slowly drizzle the warmed milk, about a teaspoon at first, then a little more each time, into the blender. Blend on low speed to combine.

4 Pour the mixture into 6 individual ramekins, filling them about two-thirds full. Chill them in the fridge for at least 2 hours or up to 6 hours.

5 Serve the mousse as is or with a scoop of Vanilla Coconut Ice Cream on top.

Seeded Dark Chocolate–Almond Bark

Layers of dark chocolate and almond butter sprinkled with crunchy seeds offer the perfect sweetness for a light bite after dinner or even for a yummy snack. —*Mike* **Makes about 20 pieces**

¼ cup pure maple syrup

2 tablespoons virgin coconut oil, melted

1 teaspoon pure vanilla extract

⅓ cup dried currants (or raisins)

½ cup gluten-free rolled oats

Pinch of pink Himalayan salt

½ cup raw cashews, chopped

½ cup walnut halves, chopped

2 tablespoons hemp seeds

2 tablespoons chia seeds

2 tablespoons flaxseed

2 tablespoons sesame seeds

1 cup raw almond butter

1 cup dark chocolate chips

1   Preheat the oven to 350°F. Line a small baking sheet with parchment paper.

2   In a large bowl, mix the maple syrup, coconut oil, vanilla, currants, oats, salt, cashews, walnuts, hemp seeds, chia seeds, flaxseed, and sesame seeds together until well combined. Spread the mixture evenly over the prepared baking sheet, forming a thin layer. Bake for 20 minutes, until golden brown and hardened. Let this base cool slightly on the baking sheet for at least 10 minutes.

3   Spread the almond butter over the base and set it aside.

4   Place the chocolate chips in a glass or other heat-safe bowl. Place the bowl over a saucepan of simmering water (do not let the bowl touch the water) and allow the chocolate chips to melt completely, stirring them occasionally. Remove the bowl from the saucepan, and drizzle the melted chocolate over the bark, smoothing it with a spatula. Place the baking sheet in the fridge for 20 minutes for the bark to set.

5   Remove the bark and break it into pieces. Store the pieces in an airtight container in the fridge for up to 2 weeks or in the freezer for up to 1 month.

Vanilla Honey Marshmallows

Some of my favorite childhood memories revolve around marshmallows: the holidays with a warm cup of hot chocolate and marshmallows on the top, or making s'mores in the summer. I like re-creating those memories with my kids, but I had to find a recipe for a healthier marshmallow.

It's really important to get your liquid to 235°F here; otherwise these won't work. Make sure you have a candy thermometer on hand. **Makes 35 marshmallows**

1 cup plus 2 tablespoons raw honey   3 tablespoons unflavored gelatin   ½ teaspoon pure vanilla extract

1 Line a medium baking sheet with parchment paper and set it aside.

2 In a small saucepan, bring ½ cup of water and the honey to a simmer over medium heat. Using an instant-read thermometer, bring the mixture to 235°F (this step is very important—the heat has to be right for this to work). This is called the soft ball stage (when the bubbles continue to get smaller as the honey and water cook together) and will take about 10 minutes to reach.

3 Meanwhile, pour ½ cup of water into the bowl of a stand mixer and sprinkle the gelatin over the top; let it sit for 5 minutes for the gelatin to "bloom." (You can tell the gelatin is starting to bloom once it starts to thicken and absorb the water.)

4 Once the gelatin has bloomed and looks like a loose form of jelly, attach the whisk to your stand mixer, and with the mixer running on medium speed, slowly pour the hot honey mixture down the side of the mixing bowl while gradually raising the speed to high. Continue to beat for 15 minutes, until you start to see the mixture turn white and fluff up and the bowl get cold. Then mix in the vanilla and whisk for 10 more seconds, until just combined.

5 Working quickly, use a rubber spatula to scrape down the sides of the bowl while dumping the marshmallow mixture onto the prepared baking sheet. Before it starts to set, smooth the mixture out. Once it is smooth, allow it to rest for 30 minutes to fully firm up.

6 Cut into squares and enjoy the marshmallows right away, or store them in an airtight container at room temperature for up to 1 week.

Chocolate Pistachio-Crusted Figs

Figs are naturally sweet, and when paired with chocolate and pistachios, they give a nice crunch. These are great when you need a little something for dessert (or just a sweet snack). Chocolate-dipped strawberries better watch out. **Makes 14 covered figs**

½ cup dark chocolate chips
1 teaspoon virgin coconut oil

¼ cup chopped pistachios
14 fresh Mission figs

Flaky sea salt, such as Maldon

1   Line a large baking sheet with parchment paper. Set it aside.

2   Place the chocolate chips and coconut oil in a glass or other heat-safe bowl. Place the bowl over a saucepan of simmering water (do not let the bowl touch the water) and allow the chocolate chips and coconut oil to melt completely, stirring them occasionally. Remove the bowl from the saucepan.

3   Place the pistachios in a shallow dish.

4   Holding it by the stem, dip a fig in the chocolate, covering as much of the fig as possible. Then roll the fig in the pistachios. Place it on the prepared baking sheet and repeat with the remaining figs. Sprinkle each fig with sea salt. Place the baking sheet in the fridge for at least 1 hour to allow the coating to harden.

5   Enjoy the figs right away or store them in an airtight container in the fridge for up to 5 days.

Dairy- and Gluten-Free Pumpkin Pie

Everyone has a pumpkin pie recipe (or at least has easy access to one). There's nothing groundbreaking here except that this is a healthier version than the one you might be used to. **Serves 8**

Crust

2 tablespoons virgin coconut oil, plus more for the pie dish, melted

1½ cups oat flour

3 teaspoons arrowroot powder

2 tablespoons coconut sugar

½ teaspoon baking powder

⅛ teaspoon baking soda

¼ teaspoon pink Himalayan salt

1 teaspoon ground cinnamon

1 egg, beaten

1 teaspoon pure vanilla extract

1 teaspoon cashew butter

1 teaspoon pure maple syrup

Filling

3 eggs

1 (15-ounce) can pumpkin puree

½ cup full-fat coconut milk

1 teaspoon pure vanilla extract

¾ cup coconut sugar

½ teaspoon pink Himalayan salt

1 teaspoon ground cinnamon

¼ teaspoon ground nutmeg

⅛ teaspoon ground ginger

Pinch of ground allspice

Optional Topping

Vanilla Coconut Ice Cream (page 217)

1 **Make the crust:** Preheat the oven to 400°F. Grease a pie dish with coconut oil.

2 In a food processor, combine 1 cup of the oat flour with the arrowroot powder, coconut sugar, baking powder, baking soda, salt, and cinnamon, and pulse until combined. Add the coconut oil, egg, vanilla, cashew butter, and maple syrup, and pulse again to combine.

3 Making sure to scrape down the sides of the processor, transfer the mixture to a large bowl. Add the remaining ½ cup oat flour and fold it in until the mixture is combined and resembles a dough. Press it into the prepared pie dish and bake for 13 minutes.

4 **Meanwhile, make the filling:** In a high-powered blender, combine the eggs, pumpkin puree, coconut milk, vanilla, coconut sugar, salt, cinnamon, nutmeg, ginger, and allspice. Blend until completely smooth.

5 Pour the filling into the pie crust, return it to the oven, and bake for 45 minutes, until the center is set.

6 Remove the pie from the oven and let it rest for at least 30 minutes. Then serve it immediately, with Vanilla Coconut Ice Cream (if desired). Or place the pie in the fridge for at least 2 hours to serve chilled. Pie will keep well in the fridge up to 4 days (if it will last that long!).

Affogato Two Ways

A traditional Italian dessert, an *affogato* is vanilla ice cream or gelato "drowned" with a shot of hot espresso. These are great for a light jolt after a big meal. If I consume espresso after dinner, I won't sleep, so here I'm giving you both a traditional recipe and one made with matcha. The matcha version won't keep me up at night and tastes just as good—plus it's green, perfect for the holidays or St. Patrick's Day. **Serves 1**

MATCHA AFFOGATO

1 cup almond or coconut milk

1 teaspoon matcha powder

1 teaspoon pure maple syrup

¼ teaspoon pure vanilla extract

1 cup Vanilla Coconut Ice Cream (page 217)

1 In a small saucepan, combine the milk, matcha powder, maple syrup, and vanilla. Whisk the mixture over medium-high heat until well combined. Let it chill in the fridge for 30 minutes, or pour it over ice to chill it quickly.

2 Place the ice cream in a glass and pour the matcha over it. Enjoy right away!

ESPRESSO AFFOGATO

1 cup hot brewed coffee or espresso

1 teaspoon pure maple syrup (optional)

1 cup Vanilla Coconut Ice Cream (page 217)

1 In a small pitcher, stir the coffee with the maple syrup (if using). Let the mixture chill in the fridge for 30 minutes, or pour it over ice to chill it quickly.

2 Place the ice cream in a glass and pour the coffee over it. Enjoy right away!

Peanut Butter
Rice Crispy Bars

To say that we are a peanut butter—loving family would be an understatement. I like peanut butter best when it's paired with chocolate because, honestly, there's no better combo. These bars have a nice crispy crunch and the chocolate and peanut butter will make it hard for you to eat just one. **Makes about 24 bars**

2 cups chunky peanut butter, at room temperature

2 cups smooth peanut butter, at room temperature

¼ cup coconut sugar

1 tablespoon pure maple syrup

2 tablespoons plus ¼ cup virgin coconut oil, melted

8 cups brown rice crispy cereal

2 cups dark chocolate chips

1 tablespoon coconut cream

¼ teaspoon pink Himalayan salt

1   Line a large baking sheet with parchment paper and set it aside.

2   In a large mixing bowl, combine both peanut butters with the coconut sugar, maple syrup, and the 2 tablespoons coconut oil. Add the brown rice cereal and stir to combine. Spread the peanut butter mixture out on the prepared baking sheet, pressing the mixture to the edges. Chill in the fridge for 20 minutes.

3   Meanwhile, combine the chocolate chips, the remaining ¼ cup coconut oil, the coconut cream, and the salt in a glass or other heat-safe bowl. Place the bowl over a saucepan of simmering water (do not let the bowl touch the water) and allow the mixture to completely melt and blend together, stirring it occasionally.

4   Remove the bowl from the saucepan and pour the mixture over the peanut butter base, spreading it edge to edge with a rubber spatula.

5   Return the baking sheet to the fridge and let the bar chill until set, 30 minutes. Then cut it into individual bars.

6   The bars will keep well in an airtight container in the fridge for up to 2 weeks.

Dark Chocolate Peppermint French Silk Pie

One of the most popular flavor combos ever, chocolate and peppermint has been a favorite of mine since I was a little girl. Silk pies are rich yet light and seemingly (but not really) elaborate, perfect for entertaining. There won't be any leftovers, so if you want some the next day, I recommend making two! I make this a day ahead since it takes a few hours—or you can make it first thing on the morning of your gathering. **Serves 8**

Crust

½ cup oat flour, plus more for the work surface

¾ cup almond flour

2 tablespoons arrowroot powder

1 egg yolk

¼ cup coconut sugar

⅛ teaspoon pink Himalayan salt

3 tablespoons virgin coconut oil

1 tablespoon almond milk

Virgin coconut oil, for the pie dish

Filling

2 cups coconut cream

2 tablespoons arrowroot powder

1 tablespoon raw cacao powder

¼ cup coconut sugar

1 tablespoon raw honey

½ teaspoon unflavored gelatin

⅔ cup dark chocolate chips

¼ cup semisweet chocolate chips

1 tablespoon virgin coconut oil

½ teaspoon pure vanilla extract

1 teaspoon peppermint extract

1 **Make the crust:** In a medium bowl, stir together the oat flour, almond flour, arrowroot powder, egg yolk, coconut sugar, and salt until combined. Add the coconut oil and mix until little crumbs start to form. Then add the almond milk, 1 teaspoon at a time, mixing until a dough begins to form. Place the dough on a lightly floured work surface and knead it with your hands until it comes together (don't be alarmed if this dough isn't as firm as other doughs—it shouldn't be). Chill the dough wrapped in plastic wrap in the refrigerator for 20 minutes.

(recipe continues)

2 Meanwhile, preheat the oven to 350°F and grease an 8-inch pie dish with the coconut oil.

3 Carefully press the chilled dough into the prepared pie dish. Crimp the edges and prick the dough all over with a fork. Bake for 15 minutes. Then remove the crust from the oven and set it aside to cool for at least 25 minutes.

4 **Make the filling:** In a medium saucepan, combine the coconut cream, arrowroot powder, cacao powder, coconut sugar, and honey. Bring to a simmer over medium heat and stir until well combined, 4 minutes. Add the gelatin, whisking constantly until it is completely combined. Then continue to cook until the filling is smooth and slightly thickened, 5 minutes.

5 Remove the saucepan from the heat and add the dark chocolate chips, semisweet chocolate chips, coconut oil, vanilla, and peppermint. Whisk until all the chocolate has melted and the mixture is silky smooth, 2 minutes.

6 Pour the mixture into the piecrust. Chill the pie uncovered in the fridge until it is completely set, about 3 hours, or in the freezer for 2 hours, before serving.

Thumbprint Cookies

My children love this healthy take on a classic holiday cookie. They're not overly sweet, so grab one when you just want a little something. **Makes 14 cookies**

1¼ cups almond flour

½ cup arrowroot powder

2 eggs

½ teaspoon pink Himalayan salt

1 tablespoon virgin coconut oil, melted

½ cup coconut sugar

3 tablespoons oat flour

½ cup jelly of choice (I like raspberry)

1 In a stand mixer, combine the almond flour, arrowroot powder, eggs, salt, coconut oil, coconut sugar, and oat flour; mix until well combined. If the dough is too dry, gradually add a little water; or if it's too sticky, add more oat flour. The dough should be sticky but not so much that it sticks to your fingers. Wrap the dough in plastic wrap and chill it in the fridge for 2 hours or up to overnight.

2 When you are ready to bake the cookies, preheat the oven to 325°F and line a large baking sheet with parchment paper.

3 Using your hands, roll portions of the dough into balls the size of a golf ball; place them on the prepared baking sheet. Press down on each ball with your thumb, creating a little indentation. Fill each well with jelly, about 2 teaspoons per cookie.

4 Bake until the cookies are golden brown, 10 to 12 minutes. Let them cool on a wire rack for 10 minutes before eating.

5 These keep well in an airtight container on the counter for up to 5 days.

Avocado Chocolate Cookies
with Sea Salt

Avocados are so versatile that they're even good for baking—they make desserts creamy and thick without being overpowering. Plus, avocados are health powerhouses full of good fats, potassium, and fiber. These cookies are ever-so-slightly gooey, in the most perfect way. **Makes 18 cookies**

½ large avocado, chopped

½ cup oat flour

2 eggs

½ cup raw cacao powder

½ cup pure maple syrup

1 teaspoon pure vanilla extract

½ teaspoon baking powder

½ teaspoon pink Himalayan salt

Flaky sea salt, such as Maldon

1   Preheat the oven to 350°F. Line a large baking sheet with parchment paper.

2   In a high-powered blender, combine the avocado, oat flour, eggs, cacao powder, maple syrup, vanilla, baking powder, and salt. Blend until completely smooth, 2 minutes.

3   Spoon the batter onto the prepared baking sheet, about 1 tablespoon per cookie. Bake for 8 minutes, until a toothpick inserted in the center of a cookie comes out clean. Let the cookies cool for 10 minutes on a wire rack before eating.

4   The cookies will keep well in an airtight container on the counter for up to 5 days.

Vanilla Coconut
Ice Cream

This recipe requires an ice cream maker, but it's so worth it. The ice cream keeps well in the freezer for up to 2 weeks, but it's best eaten right away for its velvety creaminess. I like changing up the extra ingredients I add to flavor the ice cream, but my go-tos are peppermint oil and chocolate chips or chunks of cookie dough. Feel free to use your own favorites, adding them to the finished ice cream. I'll keep it plain (as the recipe is) when serving it with pumpkin pie (page 206), in the *affogato* variations (page 209), or with warm apple pie. **Makes about 1 pint**

1 cup full-fat coconut milk

2 cups coconut cream

½ cup pure maple syrup

¼ teaspoon pink Himalayan salt

1 tablespoon pure vanilla extract

1 In a high-powered blender, combine the coconut milk, coconut cream, maple syrup, salt, and vanilla. Blend until smooth and creamy, 1 minute.

2 Transfer the mixture to an ice cream mixer and mix according to the manufacturer's directions, until it's cold and creamy and no more liquid is present.

3 Transfer the ice cream to a bowl and serve it right away, or store it in the freezer for up to 2 weeks.

Drinks

Pumpkin Spice Latte

It seems like every year Starbucks brings their pumpkin spice lattes back a week or two earlier because there's such a demand for them. I used to be one of their biggest fans before I discovered what's really in them: Did you know they don't contain any real pumpkin? It's all additives to emulate pumpkin flavor. Since I'm all about using real ingredients, I decided to figure out a way to re-create this heavenly drink so we can enjoy it once the leaves start falling off the trees. **Serves 2**

2 cups full-fat coconut milk

4 shots espresso

2 tablespoons Pumpkin Spice Syrup (recipe follows)

1 In a small saucepan, warm the coconut milk over medium heat for 2 minutes. Add the espresso and the Pumpkin Spice Syrup, whisking to combine. Let the mixture cook for 2 minutes, until the flavors have combined and the drink is simmering.

2 Divide the pumpkin spice latte between 2 mugs and serve right away.

PUMPKIN SPICE SYRUP

Makes about 1 cup

⅓ cup canned pumpkin puree

½ teaspoon ground cinnamon

¼ teaspoon ground nutmeg

⅛ teaspoon ground cloves

½ teaspoon vanilla bean powder

1½ cups coconut sugar

1 In a small saucepan, combine the pumpkin, cinnamon, nutmeg, cloves, vanilla powder, coconut sugar, and 1 cup water, and whisk together well. Bring to a boil, then reduce to a simmer for 10 minutes, stirring occasionally, until the mixture thickens substantially.

2 You can store the syrup in an airtight container in the fridge for up to 1 month.

Cashew Eggnog

Eggnog is one of the most luxurious drinks there is, especially when it's made with brandy or bourbon (although I actually prefer it without alcohol). This version is rich and creamy, the perfect drink to usher in the holiday spirit, and just as good without any dairy. **Serves 6**

2 cups cashew milk

1 tablespoon pure maple syrup

3 eggs

⅓ cup coconut sugar

1 cup coconut cream

½ teaspoon ground nutmeg, plus more for serving

1 teaspoon ground cinnamon

1 teaspoon pure vanilla extract

1 In a small saucepan, bring the cashew milk and maple syrup to a slow simmer over medium heat. Remove the pan from the heat and set it aside.

2 Separate the egg yolks and whites, placing them in separate large mixing bowls. Whisk the egg yolks with the coconut sugar until the mixture becomes light and smooth, about 3 minutes. Add the coconut cream and mix to combine.

3 Slowly whisk the hot cashew milk into the egg yolk mixture, making sure to whisk the entire time so the eggs don't curdle. Once the mixture is completely smooth, add the nutmeg, cinnamon, and vanilla. (Pass the mixture through a fine-mesh strainer if needed.)

4 In a stand mixer or with a handheld mixer, beat the egg whites until they reach medium peaks, 5 minutes. Whisk the beaten whites into the warm milk mixture until combined.

5 Pour the eggnog into a large mason jar or other airtight container and place it in the fridge to chill completely before serving, at least 1 hour or up to 1 day.

6 Before serving, give the mason jar a good shake. Garnish each serving of eggnog with a sprinkle of ground nutmeg. The nog will keep well in the fridge up to 3 days.

Peppermint Mocha

Before I started eating healthy, I would be at Starbucks almost every single day in the colder months to buy myself a peppermint mocha. Starbucks's mochas are loaded with sugar and their syrups have additives I'm not crazy about, but the flavor combo is still my weakness. Now I make them at home so I know exactly what's going into my drink. **Serves 1**

½ cup full-fat coconut milk

1 to 2 shots espresso

1 tablespoon raw cacao powder

1 teaspoon pure maple syrup

¼ teaspoon peppermint extract

In a small saucepan, warm the coconut milk over medium-high heat to your desired temperature. Pour the warmed milk into a high-powered blender and add the espresso, cacao powder, maple syrup, and peppermint. Blend until the drink is combined and slightly frothy, about 1 minute. Pour it into a mug and enjoy it immediately.

Reishi Latte

I enjoy constantly changing up what I put in my coffee, and my current obsession is reishi (a mushroom with a ton of health benefits). Reishi powder is known to boost the immune system and fight fatigue. He Shou Wu powder is an herbal remedy used to promote healthy aging. So that means I'll have another latte! **Serves 1**

1 cup almond milk

¾ teaspoon reishi powder

½ teaspoon He Shou Wu powder

1 teaspoon raw cacao powder

1 teaspoon virgin coconut oil

¼ teaspoon ground cinnamon

1 teaspoon pure maple syrup

¼ teaspoon pure vanilla extract

1 to 2 shots brewed espresso

Pinch of pink Himalayan salt

In a small saucepan, whisk the almond milk with the reishi, He Shou Wu, and cacao powders. Stir in the coconut oil, cinnamon, maple syrup, vanilla, espresso, and salt. Place the pan over medium heat and cook, stirring occasionally, until the latte simmers, 5 minutes. Serve right away.

Mint Chlorella Latte

I love coffee—there's no doubt about it. But I also use coffee as a way to get some extra nutrients in from time to time. Here I've added chlorella powder for its incredible health benefits, which include boosting the immune system. A few mint extract drops make this the perfect holiday latte. **Serves 1**

1 ½ cups almond milk

1 teaspoon ground cinnamon

½ teaspoon chlorella powder

1 teaspoon pure vanilla extract

1 teaspoon raw honey

¼ teaspoon peppermint extract

2 shots espresso

In a small saucepan, combine the almond milk with the cinnamon, chlorella powder, vanilla, honey, peppermint extract, and espresso. Warm the mixture over medium heat to your desired temperature, whisking until combined. Drink immediately.

Rosemary Charcoal Latte

My favorite breakfast spot in Nashville has a charcoal latte on its menu, and when I first saw it, I thought it was the coolest idea. Charcoal is all the rage because it draws out toxins from the body. You can't taste it here—you just reap all the health benefits. **Serves 1**

1 cup full-fat coconut milk

¼ teaspoon activated charcoal (from about 2 capsules)

¼ teaspoon finely chopped fresh rosemary

1 to 2 shots espresso

1 teaspoon pure maple syrup

In a small saucepan, warm the coconut milk over medium-high heat to your desired temperature. Pour the warmed milk into a high-powered blender and add the charcoal, rosemary, espresso, and maple syrup. Blend until combined and slightly frothy, about 1 minute. Pour into a mug and enjoy.

Cortado

A traditional *cortado*, originally from Spain, is espresso mixed
with equal parts milk. If that doesn't speak my language, then
I don't know what does. Normally a latte girl, I need an extra
jolt to get going in the gray, cold winter months. That's when I
add that extra shot of espresso and, voilà! I'm drinking a fancy
cortado. **Serves 1**

¼ cup full–fat coconut milk

¼ cup almond milk

½ cup brewed espresso
(about 3 shots)

Sweetener of choice
(I like a splash of maple syrup)

In a small saucepan, combine the coconut milk
and almond milk, and warm the mixture over
medium-high heat to your desired temperature.
Add the espresso and sweetener, and whisk
until combined. Pour into a mug and enjoy.

Apple Cider

The smell and taste of apple cider evoke fall so well. I love making this because when I do, my entire house smells amazing. I have the best memories of sitting outside with my kids on crisp evenings while we sip on this apple cider. **Makes about 4 cups**

10 apples, such as Fuji or Gala, quartered but not peeled or cored

½ cup coconut sugar

1 tablespoon ground cinnamon

1 tablespoon ground allspice

1   Place the apples in a large pot and add water until it covers the apples by about 1 inch. Bring the water to a boil. Then stir in the sugar, cinnamon, and allspice. Reduce the heat to a low boil and cook, uncovered, for 1 hour. Then cover the pot, reduce the heat further, and simmer for another 2 hours.

2   Pour the cider through a fine-mesh strainer into a large bowl or pitcher, working in batches if needed. Discard the solids (or save them to make apple butter).

3   Place the cider in the fridge and let it cool completely, or enjoy it right away while it's still warm. It will keep well in the fridge for up to 1 week.

TAHINI-SPICED
HOT COCOA

APPLE
CIDER

VANILLA CHAI
LATTE

Vanilla Chai Latte

I like this chai for an afternoon pick-me-up. If I drink coffee past noon, I'll be up all night, so this chai latte does the trick and still allows me to fall asleep at a normal hour. **Serves 2**

2 black tea bags

2 cups full-fat coconut milk

1 teaspoon raw honey

1 teaspoon pure maple syrup

½ teaspoon ground cinnamon

¼ teaspoon ground ginger

¼ teaspoon ground cardamom

¼ teaspoon ground nutmeg

¼ teaspoon ground cloves

1 teaspoon pure vanilla extract

1   Steep both tea bags in 1 cup of hot water for 5 minutes. Remove and discard the tea bags.

2   Meanwhile, warm the coconut milk in a small saucepan over medium-high heat to your desired temperature.

3   Pour the warmed coconut milk into a high-powered blender and add the brewed tea, honey, maple syrup, cinnamon, ginger, cardamom, nutmeg, cloves, and vanilla. Blend until the latte is combined and slightly frothy, about 1 minute.

4   Pour into 2 mugs and enjoy.

Tahini-Spiced Hot Cocoa

There's nothing like a cup of hot chocolate in the middle of winter; it reminds me of being a kid. Tahini adds a slightly nutty flavor to this cup of goodness, and it's full of antioxidants, vitamins, and minerals. My favorite thing to make after the kids and I go for a brisk walk on a cool day, it instantly warms us up. **Serves 1**

1 ½ cups almond milk

2 ½ teaspoons pure vanilla extract

½ teaspoon ground cinnamon

1 tablespoon raw cacao powder

1 ½ teaspoons raw honey

3 teaspoons tahini

In a small saucepan, warm the almond milk over medium-high heat until it simmers, 5 minutes. Pour the warmed milk into a high-powered blender and add the vanilla, cinnamon, cacao powder, honey, and tahini. Blend on high speed until the cocoa is smooth and frothy; 1 minute. Drink right away.

Recharge Smoothie

The colder months sometimes lead to more indulging, so I like to reset every once in a while to get back on track and make sure I'm still getting good nutrients. I love this smoothie for just that reason. It's loaded with vitamins and minerals and will give you a good boost. Frozen cauliflower is one of my favorite secret ingredients for smoothies: it makes them creamy without adding any sugar. Brain octane oil is a fat that's extracted from the most potent part of the coconut and is converted into brain-fueling, fat-burning ketone energy. Feel free to leave it out if you don't have any or just don't want to use it. **Serves 1**

½ avocado

1 tablespoon raw honey

1 cup almond milk

2 tablespoons raw cacao nibs

1 cup frozen cauliflower florets

1 big handful fresh spinach

1 teaspoon brain octane oil (optional; I like Bulletproof)

1 tablespoon bee pollen

1 tablespoon hemp seeds

¼ cup chopped or sliced blueberries and blackberries

Place the avocado, honey, almond milk, cacao nibs, cauliflower, spinach, and brain octane oil (if using) in a high-powered blender and blend until well combined, about 1 minute. Pour the mixture into a glass and top with the bee pollen, hemp seeds, and berries. Enjoy right away.

Turmeric Lemon Anti-inflammatory Smoothie

Turmeric is incredible for the immune system, so I try to incorporate it into any recipes I can. This smoothie is light and refreshing and packed with good nutrients. Frozen banana makes it creamy, while lemon and turmeric reset your system. **Serves 1**

1 frozen banana

¼ cup frozen cauliflower florets

1 teaspoon ground turmeric

Juice of 1 medium lemon

1 teaspoon raw honey

1 cup almond milk or full-fat coconut milk

¼ teaspoon ground ginger, or 1¼-inch–thick slice of fresh ginger, peeled

Bee pollen, for serving

In a high-powered blender, combine the banana, cauliflower, turmeric, lemon juice, honey, almond milk, and ginger. Blend on high speed until completely smooth, about 1 minute. Pour the smoothie into a tall glass and sprinkle bee pollen over the top. Enjoy right away.

Coffee Kick Smoothie

What better way to start your morning than with coffee and a smoothie all in one? This drink is so good, it should almost be a dessert. You can also pour it into popsicle molds for a yummy adult treat in the summer. Hidden cauliflower makes this smoothie super-creamy without adding any flavor—my secret ingredient! **Serves 1**

1 tablespoon ground coffee or instant coffee granules

1 tablespoon raw cacao powder

1 tablespoon coconut cream

1 cup frozen cauliflower florets

1 ½ cups almond milk

1 frozen banana

Place the coffee, cacao powder, coconut cream, cauliflower, almond milk, and banana in a high-powered blender and blend until well combined, about 1 minute. Pour into a tall glass and enjoy.

Lemon Cayenne Elixir

With three kids at school every day, colds are almost inevitable at my house during the winter. I try everything I can to fight them off when I feel them coming on. This elixir seems to keep my immune system running at its very best. **Serves 1**

Juice of 1 large lemon

1 ¼-inch-thick slice of fresh ginger, peeled and grated

¼ teaspoon cayenne pepper

1 teaspoon raw honey

In a small saucepan, combine 1½ cups of water with the lemon juice, ginger, cayenne, and honey. Warm the mixture over medium heat, whisking until it is combined and reaches your desired temperature. Drink right away.

Staples

Vanilla Almond Milk

I always have homemade almond milk in my fridge. Once you start making it, it's hard to go back to store-bought. This is a sweet version with maple syrup and vanilla, but free feel to skip those two items if you want plain almond milk (that's good for smoothies). I like this vanilla almond milk in my coffee. **Makes 4 cups**

1 cup raw almonds, soaked for 8 hours or up to overnight

2 tablespoons pure maple syrup

1 tablespoon pure vanilla extract

1 Drain and rinse the almonds. Place them in a high-powered blender and add 4 cups of filtered water, the maple syrup, and the vanilla. Blend on high speed for 1 to 2 minutes, until smooth.

2 Using a nut bag or cheesecloth, strain the milk into a large bowl. Discard the pulp or save it for biscotti, crackers, or energy bites. Store the vanilla almond milk in a glass jar in the fridge for up to 7 days.

Oat Milk

A nice change from almond milk, oat milk has an earthy flavor that mixes well in smoothies or coffee. I like switching it up between this, almond milk, and cashew milk. I find the touch of cinnamon and vanilla here to be comforting and delicious with my morning coffee, but you can leave this plain if you don't want any sweetener or flavor—just leave out the maple syrup, cinnamon, and vanilla. **Makes 4 cups**

4 cups gluten-free rolled oats

1 tablespoon pure maple syrup

1 teaspoon ground cinnamon

1 teaspoon pure vanilla extract

1 In a high-powered blender, stir the oats with 4 cups of filtered water. Add the maple syrup, cinnamon, and vanilla. Blend on high speed until smooth, about 1 minute. Using cheesecloth or a nut bag, strain the milk into a bowl. Discard the pulp.

2 Store the oat milk in a glass jar in the fridge for up to 5 days.

Simple Guacamole

Some things shouldn't be fussed with and one of those things is guacamole. Simple and delicious. Leave the jalapeños out if making for kids (unless yours like spicy food!). Serve the guacamole with tortilla chips. **Makes about 1½ cups**

3 avocados

½ teaspoon coarse sea salt

Juice of ½ large lime

1 teaspoon minced jalapeño (optional)

In a large bowl, combine the avocados, sea salt, lime juice, and jalapeño (if using). Mash with a fork until a few small chunks remain, or to your desired consistency.

Avocado Crema

I never make Mexican food without including this crema. It elevates every dish and makes it so I never miss the dairy in some of my favorite dishes. **Makes about 1½ cups**

1 avocado

½ cup Cashew Crema (page 259)

1 small clove garlic

Grated zest and juice of 1 lime

1 teaspoon ground cumin

½ teaspoon smoked paprika

1 teaspoon chili powder

¼ teaspoon pink Himalayan salt

1 In a high-powered blender, combine the avocado, Cashew Crema, garlic, lime zest and juice, cumin, smoked paprika, chili powder, salt, and 1 tablespoon of water. Blend on high speed until the mixture is smooth and has a thick, sauce-like consistency.

2 Transfer the crema to a serving bowl. Save crema in an airtight container up to 3 days.

Roasted Salsa

I love this salsa because it's so fresh and has a yummy charred flavor, great alone with chips or any Mexican dish like the burrito bowls with lime rice (page 74) and game day sheet pan nachos (page 77). **Makes about 2½ cups**

1 pound Roma tomatoes

½ jalapeño, seeds removed

½ red bell pepper, diced

1 clove garlic

¼ medium red onion, sliced

2 tablespoons extra-virgin olive oil

Pink Himalayan salt

¼ teaspoon ground cumin

¼ teaspoon chili powder

Juice of ½ lime

½ bunch fresh cilantro (about ½ cup loosely packed leaves)

1 Heat a grill or a grill pan over high heat.

2 On a large baking sheet, spread out the tomatoes, jalapeño, bell pepper, garlic, and onion. Sprinkle with the olive oil and toss to coat. Season with salt.

3 Place the veggies on the grill pan or directly on the grill. Grill the vegetables on each side until they are black and charred, pulling them off and returning them to the baking sheet as they are roasted: 1 to 2 minutes for the garlic, 5 to 8 minutes for the jalapeño, 8 to 9 minutes for the onion, and 10 to 12 minutes for the tomatoes and bell pepper.

4 Place the charred vegetables in a blender or food processor, and add the cumin, chili powder, lime juice, and cilantro. Blend or process until the mixture has a smooth consistency.

5 Serve the salsa warm right away, or let it cool in the fridge for at least 1 hour. It will keep well in an airtight container in the fridge for up 5 days.

Black "Refried" Beans

This black bean recipe appeared in my first cookbook, *True Roots*, but it goes so perfectly with all Mexican dishes that I had to include it in this one as well. Blending these black beans makes them velvety and incredibly comforting. You could also put these on the bottom of a salad or throw them on top of scrambled eggs for a yummy breakfast that will keep you full all morning long. **Makes about 1½ cups**

1 (15-ounce) can black beans, rinsed and drained

1 teaspoon chili powder

Pink Himalayan salt

1   In a high-powered blender, combine the beans, chili powder, a big pinch of salt, and 2 tablespoons of water; blend on high speed until smooth, using a tamp if needed.

2   Use right away, or store in an airtight container in the fridge for up to 5 days.

Pickled Red Onions

Current food obsession: anything pickled, but especially red onions. I will throw these on everything, from salads to scrambled eggs to burrito bowls. Tangy yet semi-sweet, they are a food dream. **Makes about 1 cup**

1 cup champagne vinegar

1 tablespoon raw honey

1 bay leaf

1 clove garlic

½ teaspoon red pepper flakes

½ teaspoon pink Himalayan salt

½ teaspoon freshly ground black pepper

1 large red onion, thinly sliced

1 Pour the champagne vinegar and 2 cups of water into a medium saucepan and bring to a simmer over medium-high heat. Add the honey, bay leaf, garlic, red pepper flakes, salt, and pepper; whisk to combine. Once the honey has dissolved, remove the pan from the heat.

2 Put the sliced onions in a medium bowl and pour the hot liquid over them, covering them completely.

3 Let the onions sit for at least 20 minutes at room temperature. Or for the best results, let them sit on the counter for 2 hours, then place them in the fridge, cover, and chill overnight. The pickled onions will keep well in an airtight container in the fridge for up to 1 month.

Raw Honey Mustard

I make this often because it's one of my kids' favorite condiments—they power through it, using it as a dipping sauce for every protein I cook. Obviously you can buy honey mustard at the store, but I think it tastes better homemade. **Makes about 1 cup**

⅓ cup raw honey

⅓ cup Dijon mustard

½ teaspoon champagne vinegar

½ teaspoon extra-virgin olive oil

½ teaspoon ground turmeric

¼ teaspoon pink Himalayan salt

¼ teaspoon freshly ground black pepper

1 In a small mixing bowl, whisk together the honey, mustard, vinegar, olive oil, turmeric, salt, and pepper until smooth. Transfer the mixture to an airtight container.

2 For best results, let the honey mustard chill in the fridge for 2 hours or up to overnight before using it. It will keep well in an airtight container in the fridge for up to 2 weeks.

Pickled Turmeric Eggs

One of my favorite restaurants in Nashville serves a salad with turmeric eggs, and it has changed my life. I can't even begin to describe how good I think they are. I love them on salads, but you could absolutely eat them by themselves for a snack or even for breakfast. Turmeric, a superfood, is a potent anti-inflammatory and antioxidant, a win/win. **Makes 6 eggs**

6 eggs

1 cup champagne vinegar

1 tablespoon ground turmeric

1 teaspoon pink Himalayan salt

2 cloves garlic, sliced

½ teaspoon black peppercorns

1 bay leaf

2 shallots, thinly sliced

1 jalapeño, sliced, with seeds (optional)

5 sprigs fresh thyme

1   Fill a medium saucepan with water and bring it to a boil. Add the eggs and simmer for 6 minutes. Then remove the eggs and run them under cool water until cooled completely. Shell the eggs once cooled.

2   Meanwhile, in the same medium saucepan, combine ½ cup of water with the vinegar, turmeric, salt, garlic, peppercorns, and bay leaf. Bring to a boil, then remove from the heat.

3   In a large mason jar, place the eggs, shallots, jalapeño (if using), and thyme sprigs. Pour the warm pickling liquid over the top, completely covering everything.

4   Cover the jar and let it cool to room temperature. Then place it in the fridge overnight. For the best results, let the eggs pickle for 2 days or up to a week before using. The eggs will keep well in the pickling liquid for up to 3 weeks. When you are ready to eat one (or more), simply remove the egg from the liquid and return the jar to the fridge.

PICKLED RED
ONIONS

RAW HONEY
MUSTARD

PICKLED
TURMERIC EGGS

Sweet and Tangy BBQ Sauce

I love a simple barbeque sauce that works well with all types of meat. This one is tangy with a hint of sweetness. It's also a real kid-pleaser! Great to marinate meat in or even to use as a dipping sauce. —*Mike* Makes about 1½ cups

2 cups canned tomato puree

2 tablespoons blackstrap molasses

¼ cup Worcestershire sauce

2 tablespoons apple cider vinegar

¼ teaspoon garlic powder

¼ teaspoon mustard powder

½ teaspoon onion powder

½ teaspoon smoked paprika

½ teaspoon ground ancho chile

½ teaspoon pink Himalayan salt

½ tablespoon raw honey

1 teaspoon freshly ground black pepper

1 In a medium saucepan, combine the tomato puree, molasses, Worcestershire, and vinegar. Stir in the garlic powder, mustard powder, onion powder, paprika, ground chile, salt, honey, and black pepper. Whisk in ½ cup of water and bring the mixture to a boil over medium heat. Then reduce the heat and simmer the sauce, stirring it often, until it has reduced by a third and become thicker, about 20 minutes. Remove the pan from the heat.

2 If you want the sauce to have a smoother consistency, strain it through a fine-mesh strainer into a container.

3 Serve the sauce right away or store it in an airtight container in the fridge for up to 2 weeks.

Dad's Famous Pasta Sauce

Ya gotta love a 100 percent Italian dad. Not only do I have some of the best recipes from him (and his mom, my grandma), but some of my favorite cooking memories are times in the kitchen with him when I was growing up. My dad made this sauce pictured on page 257 for the homemade meatballs on Christmas Eve. I like to make a big batch to have frozen sauce on hand for busy weeknight meals. I'll pull a bag out in the morning before I head into the office and let it defrost in the kitchen sink all day so once I come home, I just have to make some quick meatballs and boil some noodles. I also use this sauce in the slow-cooker lasagna (page 132), stuffed shells with cashew ricotta (page 109), and eggplant parmesan (page 104). **Makes about 10 cups**

3 (28-ounce) cans diced tomatoes in sauce

1 (6-ounce) can tomato paste

2 (15-ounce) cans tomato sauce

3 cloves garlic, minced

¼ cup extra-virgin olive oil

2 teaspoons dried oregano

1½ tablespoons dried basil

1 teaspoon pink Himalayan salt

Freshly ground black pepper

1   In a large saucepan, combine the diced tomatoes in sauce, tomato paste, tomato sauce, garlic, olive oil, oregano, basil, salt, and a pinch of black pepper. Stir over medium-high heat until well combined. Then simmer for at least 2 hours, uncovered, for the flavors to combine, or for up to 8 hours.

2   Use right away or freeze in ziplock bags for later use up to 3 months.

Classic Basil Pesto

I've been known to eat pesto with a spoon, and honestly, it's all I need in life to be happy. Typically, pesto is made with pine nuts, but I swap some for walnuts for a slightly tangier nutty flavor. I'll use pesto on everything from eggs to salads to pasta, and everything in between. When my kids are being stubborn about eating veggies, this is a foolproof way to get *something* green into their bodies. They love it on pasta just as much as I do. **Makes about 1¼ cups**

4 cups packed fresh basil leaves

3 tablespoons pine nuts

1 clove garlic

1 teaspoon dried oregano

⅔ cup walnut halves

Pink Himalayan salt

Freshly ground black pepper

½ cup extra-virgin olive oil

1 Combine the basil, pine nuts, garlic, oregano, walnuts, a big pinch of salt, and a pinch of pepper in a food processor and pulse until just combined.

2 With the food processor running, slowly drizzle in the olive oil. Scrape down the sides of the processor if needed.

3 Transfer the pesto to a bowl and season it with salt and pepper to taste. Use it right away or place it in an airtight container and refrigerate it for up to 1 week.

CLASSIC BASIL
PESTO

Simple Aioli

Nothing beats a homemade aioli. This is great on sandwiches and as a dip for just about anything—but especially for the parsnip fries with simple aioli (page 173). **Makes about 1 cup**

2 egg yolks

1 teaspoon Dijon mustard

¼ teaspoon fresh lemon juice

1 cup light olive oil

2 teaspoons champagne vinegar

Pink Himalayan salt

1 Place a dish towel on the counter to prevent your mixing bowl from moving, and set a large mixing bowl on top of the towel. Add the egg yolks, mustard, and lemon juice to the bowl and whisk to combine. Slowly drizzle in the olive oil, whisking vigorously for 2 to 3 minutes, until the mixture is completely combined and has thickened substantially. Add the vinegar and salt to taste, and whisk to combine (the aioli will lighten in color).

2 Chill the simple aioli in the fridge for 15 to 20 minutes before serving. It will keep well in the fridge covered up to 5 days.

Cashew Crema

Crema is known as two things: a layer of creamy froth that forms on the top of freshly made espresso (*yum*) and a heavy cream that's thickened and slightly soured, usually with buttermilk. Bottom line: it's a thick yummy cream. To have a dairy-free version of crema is a godsend. I use this cashew crema for everything from icing (with maple syrup and vanilla) to breakfast bowls (lox breakfast bowl, page 36), to soups (it makes them super-creamy). This is a dairy-free-lover's best friend. **Makes ½ cup**

1 cup raw cashews

1   Place the cashews in a high-powered blender and add ½ cup of water. Blend on high speed until the crema is completely smooth, 2 minutes.

2   The crema will keep well in an airtight container in the fridge for up to 5 days.

Orange Cranberry Jam

I've always had a passion for preserved foods, and I like to experiment combining different fruits and flavors. This jam, with its hint of cinnamon, is a unique spin on the usual strawberry or grape jam. It's perfect on toast or an English muffin. Plus, cinnamon and cranberries remind me of a traditional Thanksgiving meal. —*Mike* **Makes about 2 cups**

3 cups fresh cranberries

½ tablespoon fresh lemon juice

1 (3-inch) cinnamon stick

2 cups coconut sugar

1 cup fresh orange juice

2 large oranges

1 In a medium saucepan, combine 2 cups of water with the cranberries, lemon juice, cinnamon stick, 1 cup of the coconut sugar, and the orange juice. Bring to a simmer over medium heat, and cook until the cranberries start to blister and pop, 5 minutes. Reduce the heat to low.

2 Meanwhile, zest both oranges and then peel them, making sure not to leave any of the white pith. Using a paring knife, slice between the membranes to cut the oranges into segments, discarding any seeds. Combine the orange segments and the remaining 1 cup coconut sugar with the cooked cranberries.

3 Bring the mixture to a boil. Reduce the heat and simmer for 1 hour, stirring occasionally, until the jam has thickened. Remove the pan from the heat and let the jam cool completely. Remove the cinnamon stick, then transfer the jam to a bowl, cover, and chill in the refrigerator for at least 2 hours. The jam will thicken up the longer it cools (overnight for the best results).

4 The jam keeps well in an airtight container in the fridge for up to 1 month.

Classic Caesar Dressing

Homemade Caesar dressing reminds me of my dad. I'll never forget the first time I had this dressing, which he made with anchovies (before that, I thought anchovies were disgusting). We were on vacation in Turks and Caicos, and I helped him make what will forever remain in my memory as the best salad I've ever had. **Makes about 1 cup**

5 medium cloves garlic, minced

1 tablespoon Dijon mustard

1 tablespoon champagne vinegar

Pink Himalayan salt

Freshly ground black pepper

2 tablespoons vegan mayo

½ cup extra-virgin olive oil

Juice of ½ lemon

4 small oil–packed anchovies, minced

In a medium bowl, whisk together the garlic, mustard, and vinegar. Add a big pinch of salt and a pinch of pepper. Then add the mayo, olive oil, lemon juice, and anchovies, and stir to combine. Add more salt and pepper if needed. Keeps well in an airtight container in the fridge up to 1 week.

Ranch Dressing

This ranch dressing recipe comes from my first book, *Balancing in Heels*. It has been my go-to dressing for more than 5 years and I don't see that changing anytime soon. I like vegan mayo for the subtle flavor, but feel free to use your favorite. **Makes about 2 cups**

1½ cups vegan mayo

¼ cup plain almond milk (see page 242)

1 tablespoon apple cider vinegar

1 tablespoon fresh chopped parsley

1½ teaspoons onion powder

1 teaspoon garlic powder

½ teaspoon dried dill

¼ teaspoon freshly ground black pepper

1   In a high-powered blender, combine the mayo, almond milk, vinegar, parsley, onion powder, garlic powder, dill, and black pepper. Blend until combined and creamy.

2   The dressing keeps well in an airtight container in the fridge for up to 10 days.

Acknowledgments

First and foremost, thank you to my fans. It's because of you guys that I'm able to do the things I love, and this cookbook (like my first cookbook, *True Roots*) is such a passion project of mine. Being able to connect through food is a dream come true.

I couldn't have written this book without the support of some very special people. Mike, I loved having you back in my kitchen for so many months while we tested and tested and came up with so many delicious ideas together. I continue to learn and grow in the kitchen and it's all because of you. I miss having you around, but I'm hoping we will be back for another one!

To my three angels, Camden, Jaxon, and Saylor: Thanks for being my inspiration in everything I do and for giving me real purpose in this life. You guys made recipe testing more fun by joining me in the kitchen and always wanting to be part of the madness. I love that you three are always up for helping me cook and bake. Plus, you're my brutally honest taste testers, which is a very important role!

Dad, how cool that your meatballs are published! Woohoo! Thanks for all the tips and tricks and ideas for this book. As an Italian, you'll see that this book is right up your alley! I couldn't have done it without you.

Mom, thanks for always supporting everything I do, no matter how big or small. You taught me how to bake at a young age, and I continue to do that with my kids and always think of you when I do. Some of my favorite memories are my times with you in the kitchen.

To Dervla Kelly and everyone at Penguin Random House, including Mia Johnson, Abby Oladipo, Jane Chinn, Merri Ann Morrell, Neil Spitkovsky, Nicholas Patton, Brianne Sperber, and Tammy Blake, thank you for giving me another opportunity to share my recipes with the world. This has been such an incredibly fun journey and you've been behind me always. That means the world.

Susan, Jack, and Margaret—for all you do.

Much Love.

Index

RODALE and the Plant colophon are
registered trademarks of Penguin
Random House LLC.

Library of Congress Cataloging-in-
Publication Data
Names: Cavallari, Kristin, 1987–author.
Title: True comfort / Kristin Cavallari.
Description: First edition. | New York
    : Rodale, 2020. | Includes index. |
    Identifiers: LCCN 2019046137
    (print) | LCCN 2019046138
    (ebook) | ISBN 9781984826282 |
    ISBN 9781984826299 (ebook)
Subjects: LCSH: Comfort food. |
    Cooking, American. | LCGFT:
    Cookbooks
Classification: LCC TX740 .C39 2020
    (print) | LCC TX740 (ebook) | DDC
    641.3—dc23
LC record available at https://lccn.loc.
    gov/2019046137
LC ebook record available at https://
    lccn.loc.gov/2019046138

ISBN 978-1-9848-2628-2
Ebook ISBN 978-1-9848-2629-9
Target ISBN 978-0-593-23248-4

Printed in China

Book and cover design by Mia Johnson
Photographs by Aubrie Pick

10 9 8 7 6 5 4 3 2 1

First Edition